Clocking Out Early

The Ultimate Guide to Early Retirement

By Cody and Georgi Boorman

For Eloise

Table of Contents

Introduction   5
Ch 1: The Big Cost of Little Things   8
Ch 2: Reforming Your Grocery Shopping   18
Ch 3: The Easy 3: Phone, Cable, Internet   27
Ch 4: Getting Your Money's Worth in Entertainment   34
Ch 5: Getting Around Comfortably and Cheaply   40
Ch 6: The Big One: Your Home   49
Ch 7: Minding The Meter   62
Ch 8: The True Cost of Raising Kids   72
Ch 9: Self-Care   87
Ch 10: Creating Your Surplus   96
Ch 11: Debt Payoff   103
Ch 12: Travel Hacking   110
Ch 13: Which Investments?   119
Ch 14: Don't Speculate, Invest!   129
Ch 15: Finding Your Number   134
Ch 16: Adjusting Your Number   141
Ch 17: Sequence of Return Risk   162
Ch 18: Pre-Tax Buckets   169
Ch 19: The HSA   173
Ch 20: Investment Prioritizing and Tax Harvesting   181
Ch 21: How Long Will it Take to Hit My Number?   186
Ch 22: You Hit Your Number! Now What?   192
Conclusion   213

Introduction

What if you could squirrel away a big chunk of your income every month, and ten years from now, you'd have enough money invested to generate a passive income you could live on for the rest of your life?

That option is available to you. It's not multi-level marketing. It's not playing the real estate market. It's not increasing your income with the power of positive thinking. It's just smart money management, simple investment strategies, and the power of compounding interest.

This is the FIRE path (Financially Independent, Retiring Early). A growing number of young professionals are taking an early off-ramp from the rat race—decades before traditional retirement. It is the ultimate mic-drop, an ultra-satisfying freedom, the epitome of "sticking it to the Man."

Since stumbling onto the FIRE concept in our early twenties, we've paid off over $80,000 of consumer debt and are on track to retire by 30. It's not a path we chose lightly; it takes discipline, research, and preparation. Since starting our journey, we've put thousands of hours into studying the ins and outs of early-retirement planning, and we've put the most critical knowledge and wisdom we've gained into this book.

Essentially, this is a guide to help you build your off-ramp from the traditional work-consume-work cycle of life common to most Americans. Whether you're looking to get on solid financial footing or you want to retire by 30, your budget is your vehicle for getting you wherever you want to go. If it's hauling a ton of debt and ineffective spending, any life-changing maneuvers—like losing your job, caring for a sick loved one, or prepping for an unexpected baby—will be very difficult and uncomfortable. You'll certainly never make it to your FIRE off-ramp hauling the typical American debt load and bloated budget.

In that light, the first half of this book will cover expense reduction. We'll show you how to cut costs as painlessly as possible and pay off your debt. We'll break down most of life's recurring expenses and show you how to get your annual expenses down to about $20,000 if you're single and $30,000 if you're married (plus $6,000 for your first child, followed by $2,000 for each child thereafter). This might sound impossible to you now, but we'll discuss several tips and "hacks" that will make this number feasible for most.

The latter half of the book is about constructing your off-ramp so you can stay off the congested highway of careerism: it will help you develop a plan to get you to FIRE and sustain it.

The goal is for you to build roughly 25x your annual expenses in your investment accounts. That might end up being around a million dollars, but it's very doable if you get started early. The dollars you add to your account over your investment period is only a fraction of what compound interest will produce for you.

Our aim is for Americans, especially young Americans, to learn how to buy their freedom. The earlier we can turn people on to this idea, the quicker they can get to FIRE. Time is a powerful tool in investing, and the younger you are, the more of it you have working for you.

As with most things, there are a variety of factors at play; but at its core, success is just a product of plotting your course by plugging your own income and expenses into a formula, and then sticking to your path until you reach your destination—the point at which your investments are large enough to sustain you indefinitely.

You should view any financial advice skeptically, of course, but the essential concepts of spending optimization, avoiding depreciating liabilities, paying off debt, and investing in index funds have been proven to be highly effective. Even some people in their late thirties and forties can retire well before 60 by following the principles we lay out.

This book will show you how to buy your independence from the paycheck. If your passive income is enough to sustain you indefinitely, then what life looks like once you reach FIRE is totally up to you—or at least, it's not up to an employer. You could keep your regular job, run a taco truck, travel the world, spend more time with your family, volunteer, learn how to weave baskets underwater, run for public office, or whatever the hell you want to do with your fleeting years on earth.

That's independence. That's freedom beyond anything most young Americans can imagine. If you're interested in clocking out early, this is the guide to help you do it.

Chapter 1

The Big Cost of Little Things

If you want to revolutionize your financial situation, start with the habits that are easiest to change, like "disposable income." Why do we call it that? Do we really use the same adjective for our hard-earned dollars that we use for plastic bags or paper plates?

If you have "disposable income" anywhere in your budget, you are *throwing money away.* Calling it something else doesn't change what it is—it could be "miscellaneous spending," "pocket money," or "carrying-around money." You may as well just strike that number from your budget entirely, because it isn't doing anything for you. If you must spend, spend with a purpose; don't throw it in a trash can.

What's Your Trash Can?

Popular trash cans for disposable income include fancy coffees, bar tabs, magazine subscriptions, takeout, nifty gadgets from QVC, manicures, and "I need these red heels in my life right now" purchases.

Your kids' ever-changing wants can also be trash cans for your money. We'll talk about the true cost of raising children in a later chapter, but for now, we'll leave you with a quick note: your 8 year old doesn't need an iPad for his birthday, your middle schooler doesn't need a Fitbit for Christmas, your first grader doesn't need a data plan, and none of them need soda every time you go through the drive thru.

While we're at it, let's knock out another pesky falsehood that leads to more money in the trash can: that bargains should lower the threshold of justification for a thing you do not need. Being a bargain hunter is far different, and perhaps far more dangerous, than being frugal. We all know those who score designer handbags for pennies on the dollar or grab takeout and let the food in their fridge rot because they got a two-for-one deal at the local Chinese restaurant. It doesn't matter how much the original cost of the item was; such purchases aren't good deals for your long-term financial health.

Little Purchases Keep us in the Consumerist Mindset

Every day, we're inundated with advertisements for products and services that don't increase our long-term happiness. For example, you get a dopamine rush when you buy the latest iPhone, or when you get that "good deal" on the 50% off air popcorn maker. But a month into either of those purchases, you feel about as happy as you did with the last version of the iPhone, or when you didn't have a bulky popcorn maker hogging shelf space in your kitchen. Maybe you saved 50%, but saving 100% on something you don't need is a whole lot better.

Marketers realize "getting a good deal" allows us to justify purchases we really don't need. We get sucked into an endless cycle of consumerism, buying upgrades and replacements that perform only marginally better than the things we had before, or uni-tasking gadgets and features from which we never really get our money's worth.

While buying a popcorn-maker isn't bad in and of itself, all those little things we buy, or things we spend more on than we should, add up. It's not just the cost, it's the *opportunity* cost. How could that money have been used more effectively? If you make a purchase like this every month, what happens if you instead invest the $25/month you would've wasted on whimsical purchases? In a decade, you'd have \$4,394.42.[1] That's a pretty good profit for exercising just a little self-control.

While we devote considerable time and brain power to deciding how much we want to pay for a mortgage or a new car, the small-ticket purchases are often hardly given a second thought: a new air freshener here, a box of cookies there, a garage sale haul or a pair of sunglasses. The fact that we buy everything either with cards or online with a few clicks only makes it easier to acquire needless things absentmindedly. Amazon has thousands of vendors competing for your business, and that does help keep prices lower. But think about how much less you'd spend if you did a few minutes' more research on the product you want to buy or shelved it on your wish list for a few days...You might find out that you really don't need it at all.

We aren't advocating that you shower once a week and eat Top Ramen for lunch every day. We aren't advocating that you give up hobbies that bring you enough joy to justify their expense, or that you never buy coffee at the drive thru. But the fact remains that little things add up to either big opportunity losses or big rewards in the long run, depending on how you treat them. To get your finances on solid ground, you must discover the rare skill of frugality. We call this a skill because it's not the triumph of math over present desires, as if you can check every purchase against a chart to determine whether it should be bought; rather, it is the triumph of willpower over impulse and absent-mindedness.

It was said that the British Empire was acquired in "a fit of absent-mindedness." If a whole empire can be gotten in such a frame of mind, how much more iPhones and popcorn-makers?

You must shift your frame of mind. The first step in any self-improvement project is to set a goal. The second is to become

[1]"Compound Interest Calculator" *U.S. Securities and Exchange Commission*, last modified August 25, 2016, https://www.investor.gov/additional-resources/free-financial-planning-tools/compound-interest-calculator

aware of your current state: your habits, resources, vices, and responsibilities. Once you've set the goal of paying off debt or hitting FIRE, or even a smaller goal of putting X% more of your money toward debt or retirement or some other financial goal, you can begin evaluating your situation in terms of what will bring you closer to that goal and what will push you further away from it.

You'll quickly develop a keen awareness that money, far from simply connecting you with goods and services that sustain you or symbolizing power or status, is a precious tool rather than a "disposable" resource. What do we do with good tools? We take care of them, we keep track of where they are, and we only lend them to trustworthy neighbors. We don't waste their longevity on frivolous pursuits. That is how you should treat your money. You might be surprised at how much money you have left at the end of the month when you truly value your dollar.

The fewer dollars you make with your time, the more you should value them. We all know a tightwad. Some would characterize tightwad-ism as a sign of greed or un-charitableness or even a scrooge-like distaste for life, but more likely is the prospect that he or she puts a high value on their dollars and won't part with them on a whim. This is a mindset that doesn't arise from sheer necessity (as it does in some hard economic circumstances), but comes about from the pursuit of goals that outweigh many spending habits consumerism bids us engage in.

Budget by Goal, not Percentage

Some mainstream personal finance sites recommend you allocate 5% of your net spending to "miscellaneous." Here, "miscellaneous" is the catch-all term for spending not devoted to housing, food, utilities, clothing, travel, health insurance, or entertainment. While it is prudent to make room in the budget for unexpected costs (gas money to visit a sick relative, car or home repairs, or missing a day off work), dedicating 5% of your hard-earned dollars to "miscellaneous spending" will only encourage excess spending.

The purpose of a budget should not be to set rules for yourself to keep you from overdrawing your account with absent-minded spending. A budget should be designed to:

1) Give you exact figures for how much you spend on "hard" expenses such as housing costs, phone plans, internet, gas, and loan payments.

2) Allow you to determine how much money you have left over after the hard expenses are taken care of to buy games or other "soft" expenses you may get real value from in day to day life.

3) Give you an estimate of how much you can put toward saving, paying off debt, or investing.

Articles titled "What Percentage of Your Paycheck Should You Spend Each Week" attempt to answer the wrong question. It's not about what percent you *should spend,* it's about *the minimum amount you can spend and still maintain a healthy balance between your present and future happiness.* If you feel like your budget is a set of constraints, you need to change the way you think about budgets, and possibly the way you're formulating yours. Budgets should tell you what's possible, not what isn't. It should cultivate an awareness of how much various aspects of your life cost you and help keep you on track with your goals. Ideally, it should be a reflection of your discipline, not a tyranny imposed upon your passions. But it probably won't be at first.

Estimate the Payoff of Non-Purchases

You might need to trust that a budget is for your own good and that keeping your finger off the one-click order button will pay off in the long run. That's okay. Here's a tip if you're struggling: use an online compound interest calculator to determine how much wealth you could build if you invested the small ticket amount instead of spending it now. A ballpark average interest rate is 7%, after inflation. How much will your principal produce in ten, twenty, or maybe even thirty years?

Then, start a spreadsheet with the prices of all the things you were tempted to buy. Plug the sum into the compound interest calculator after a month and see how much your self-control can gain in the long run.

Stuff I want	Price	Compounded over 10 years[2]
Popcorn maker	$24.99	$50.32
Echo (2nd gen)	$99.99	$201.34
Fitbit Flex	$59.95	$120.72
Patterned blouse	$19.98	$40.43
Commuter cup	$8.99	$18.10
Sum:		**$430.91**

It's smart to write down the things you want before buying them, wait 24 hours, and then come back to them. You'll probably find that much of your "needs" either have cheaper substitutes, can be put on the back burner until a less expensive version comes up, or foregone entirely. For instance, you might think a popcorn maker would be quite useful because popcorn is your favorite snack and you don't want to stand holding a lid over a pot until your corn is popped and risk burning it. But you also don't want to keep shelling out money on microwave popcorn. A little research might yield a "hack:" Putting kernels into a paper lunch bag with some butter and salt, folding it, and popping it in the microwave.

---

[2]"Compound Interest Calculator" *U.S. Securities and Exchange Commission*, last modified August 25, 2016, https://www.investor.gov/additional-resources/free-financial-planning-tools/compound-interest-calculator

Writing it down instead of buying it as soon as you think you need it gives you the opportunity to do some research and find creative, less expensive ways to solve your problem, or simply discover new and valuable bits of knowledge. It also safeguards you from the regret of impulse buys.

A "Big Christmas" will Cost You Big

For most families, spending gets out of control at Christmas time. Your spirit of generosity can quickly turn into a wallet-stealing poltergeist if you're not careful. All sorts of fun gadgets are justified in the month of December, from brand new computers, to sous vides, to cell phones and even new cars. Not to mention all the small ticket presents for the kids that add up to unbelievable figures. In 2017, Americans planned to spend $967.13 on average for Christmas gifts, including $330 on their children ($132 per kid on average) — and that's just for gifts.[3] Add party supplies, food, decorations, and the new trend of "self-gifting" onto that, and Americans are dropping some serious coin on a single holiday. According to a Coinstar survey from the same year, 77% of consumers expected to go over-budget.[4]

The time of year when it's hardest to control your spending is the exact time that self-restraint pays off, though. If $967.13 were your principal, to which you added about $80 a month (Christmas budget/12) and you let it compound at 7% for ten years, you'd end

---

[3]Ana Serafin Smith, "NRF Consumer Survey Points to Busy Holiday Season, Backs Up Economic Forecast and Import Numbers", *National Retail Federation*, last edited October 27, 2017, https://nrf.com/media/press-releases/nrf-consumer-survey-points-busy-holiday-season-backs-economic-forecast-and
[4]"Coinstar Holiday Survey: Results Reveal the Majority of Holiday Gift Givers Seat a Budget, Yet Hidden Expenses Put Many in the Red", *Cision PR Newswire*, last modified October 10, 2017, https://www.prnewswire.com/news-releases/coinstar-holiday-survey-results-reveal-the-majority-of-holiday-gift-givers-set-a-budget-yet-hidden-expenses-put-many-in-the-red-300533218.html

up with $15,950.99.[5] Obviously you're not going to eliminate your entire Christmas budget, but that should put things in perspective. What if you only spent half the average Christmas budget ($483.56)? You'd end up with $7,976.35 after a decade.[6] That was about the price of a 2009 Toyota Corolla in 2018.[7]

Again, it's not about deprivation: it's about thinking beyond Christmas day and weighing which things are worth your money. A few days after Christmas (or perhaps the day after), your happiness will level out. Unless you got something very useful (which should always be your aim for Christmas presents), Christmas is just a really expensive endorphin rush.

That goes for children as well. Don't give them animatronic animals or cheaply made instruments they aren't keenly interested in learning how to play. Young kids, under age 7, don't need fancy toys based off their favorite TV shows to have a good time. Imagination fuels their play, and the cardboard box their new toy came in can give them as much joy as the toy itself. After a couple weeks, the new toys will be piled in various corners of the house, abandoned. Giving like this means every few years will necessitate a garage sale to get rid of what is now classified as "junk."

If you want to get the most play out of your gifts, give them tools to be creative (crayons, washable paints, pottery wheels, window art kits) or games and puzzles, which encourage cooperation, critical thinking, and present a challenge. Give things that keep them active, like a Croquet set or a Slip N Slide they can use when the

[5] "Compound Interest Calculator" *U.S. Securities and Exchange Commission*, last modified August 25, 2016, https://www.investor.gov/additional-resources/free-financial-planning-tools/compound-interest-calculator

[6] "Compound Interest Calculator" *U.S. Securities and Exchange Commission*, last modified August 25, 2016, https://www.investor.gov/additional-resources/free-financial-planning-tools/compound-interest-calculator

[7] "10 Best Used Cars Under $8,000", *Kelley Blue Book,* last modified December 5, 2017, https://www.kbb.com/car-reviews-and-news/top-10/best-used-cars-under-8000/2100000852-4/

weather warms up—this will encourage delayed gratification, and it'll be less expensive as an off-season purchase.

Impulse food buys

Saving money might be easier if you're planning for a frugal Christmas, but what about when you see a McDonald's down the street and your stomach is growling? Food is one of the most pernicious "little things" that can cost you big. According to Business Insider, Americans on average spend over $3,000 a year on eating out, comprising a whopping 42% of their annual food budget.[8] Fast food and takeout costs can easily get out of control because often it literally *feels* like you need it, especially if you're out and about a lot or pass that Taco Bell every day on your way home from work. We'll talk more about how to manage food costs in the next chapter and how you can get your cost per meal down between $0.25-$2/person. But for now, let's look at the overall financial impact of eating out.

With item prices approaching $4-$6 at several fast food franchises and several factors of this at sit down dining establishments, we can safely assume that not eating out would at least cut that $3,000 expense in half. Assuming a standard 40 year working career, that $1,500 difference invested each year would net $330,862.13 of today's dollars 40 years from now.[9] Considering the average salary today is $44,564,[10] that fast food habit equates

[8] Alex Morrell and Skye Gould, "A close look at Americans' food budget shows an obvious place to save money", *Business Insider*, last modified February 17, 2017, http://www.businessinsider.com/americans-spending-food-bls-2017-2
[9] "Compound Interest Calculator" *U.S. Securities and Exchange Commission*, last modified August 25, 2016, https://www.investor.gov/additional-resources/free-financial-planning-tools/compound-interest-calculator
[10] "Table 3. Median usual weekly earnings of full-time wage and salary workers by age, race, Hispanic or Latino ethnicity, and sex, fourth quarter 2017 averages, not seasonally adjusted", *Bureau of Labor Statistics,* last modified January 17 2018, https://www.bls.gov/news.release/wkyeng.t03.htm

to over **seven years of work**. Is Burger King worth working an extra seven years?

Get your mindset right and the rest will follow

Now, when we say you should be careful about little purchases, we don't mean you should put your wallet on a diet. Diets are temporary and tend to be extreme. People who diet tend to commit to a diet and then quit, yo-yo-ing for years between strict regimens and lax indulgence. Generally speaking, the harder your diet is to keep, the less likely you are to stick to it. Of course, if you're 150 pounds overweight and approaching a heart attack, you better get serious and extreme. Similarly, if your financial situation is dire, you need to take all measures necessary to make it through the rough patch. But most of us come into times of plenty as well, and that's where your discipline really counts and can set you up for long-term success. Don't put your wallet on a diet; change your mindset about money and try to only purchase things that are really worth paying for.

This is especially true for recurring expenses. When you reduce or eliminate a recurring expense, it has a beautiful double effect. It both increases the surplus you have to reduce debt or increase investments, getting you to FIRE sooner, *and* reduces the amount of money you need to reach FIRE, as you no longer have to sustain that expense in retirement.

Keep this in mind when you're tempted to sign up for that recurring subscription package. Numbers can help motivate you, but financial tips, no matter how novel or wise, can't in themselves make a difference in your financial situation. Only *you* can do that. Little things can cost you big, so be aware of your spending, practice delayed gratification, and spend with a purpose.

Chapter 2

Reforming Your Grocery Shopping

In the last chapter we talked about the big cost of little things. Groceries are comprised almost completely of "little things," and so they're probably the lowest hanging fruit in terms of cost-cutting. It comprises about 12.7% of the average household budget,[11] and as previously mentioned, roughly 42% of the average food budget goes towards eating out.

This is nothing new: every personal finance book and website will tell you that the quickest way to get your food costs down is to stop eating out. Dave Ramsey is fond of saying that until you pay off your debt, you should be eating rice and beans every night (it's tongue-in-cheek...but not really).

That should be Reform Number One. We suspect the reason many people eat out is because they don't have a well-developed grocery shopping routine. If your pantry is bare and your stomach is growling, the temptation is toward immediate gratification with little effort (e.g. takeout or fast food), not to sit down and create a grocery list, then go to the store, then come home and cook dinner. No fancy cost comparison chart is going to convince a hungry and tired person to do all that thinking and work. Thus, one of the keys to reforming your grocery expenses is to set a routine for grocery shopping.

---

[11] Alex Morrell and Skye Gould, "A close look at Americans' food budget shows an obvious place to save money", *Business Insider*, last modified February 17, 2017, http://www.businessinsider.com/americans-spending-food-bls-2017-2

Prepare for the week ahead

Getting organized reduces stress by setting predictable patterns for you to follow. With routine, buying groceries is more like filling in the blanks than pulling a rabbit out of a hat. We have had the same grocery routine for years. Every Saturday, we transfer all the needed items we wrote on our little fridge whiteboard during the week (mustard, milk, eggs, etc.) to a piece of paper, and then we work out our meal plan for the week. We cook with leftovers in mind, which usually means we're cooking two to three times a week. For instance, Monday we'll make chicken burritos, which gives us leftovers for two nights; Thursday, we'll make bacon avocado burgers and eat those again on Friday (we fry all the bacon and prepare all the patties so they need only be grilled on day 2); Saturday we might bake some chicken; and Sunday is family dinner, the prep for which we rotate among Cody's parents, grandparents, and us (so every three weeks, we cook for a crowd).

Having an organized binder full of your staple meals (we categorize by protein i.e. fish, beef, chicken, etc.) is also helpful for when you just can't think of what you want for dinner that week. It's surprising how many favorite dishes we completely forget about when we don't look at our recipe binder. Having a dinner binder "remember" your meals for you, along with all the ingredients, is another stress-reliever.

We also buy our staples in bulk, such as frozen chicken, ground beef, flour, and onions, usually from Costco or WinCo. These run out about every two or three months, so most grocery trips, we don't have to worry about buying our staple foods. We also tend to get canned food in bulk when they're on sale. Keep in mind that buying perishable items in bulk might end up costing you more if you don't use them all before they go bad (think 10-pound bags of potatoes or carrots).

We write out our list of ingredients for our dinners along with anything else we've run out of, and we head to the grocery store. Our town has a Walmart, a Safeway and a WinCo. We shop at one of the three, depending on what we need. As of this writing, WinCo has excellently priced whole bean coffee. (Being from the Northwest, we're a tiny bit snobbish about our coffee and like to grind it fresh every morning.) When we're low on coffee or need bulk oatmeal, we're likely to do all our grocery shopping there. But on the weeks we run out of diapers, we'll head to Walmart, where diapers are significantly cheaper.

Optimize your trip

We like to organize the items on our list by area of the store, which optimizes the trip. This is especially stress-relieving if you have a baby or toddler who gets cranky in the store after a short period of time. It also keeps you from roaming down aisles that coax more money out of your wallet (the cookie aisle or cosmetics aisle, for example). It's been our experience that the more time you spend in a store and the less sure you are about what you need for the coming week, the more likely you are to buy things that aren't on your list or forget an item that you do need.

So, establish a routine, be prepared, have a purpose and optimize your trip. The more regularly you shop for groceries (we mean by regular intervals, not frequency - many people shop once a month, save for produce, and do just fine), the easier it is to avoid takeout temptation. A well-prepared list will also cut down on extra trips back to the store, or to a closer store that's more expensive (Whole Foods, for instance), to get something you forgot.

That said, you're still going to face those times when you're out running errands, and for whatever reason you're hungry and cranky and can't focus on completing the rest of your tasks. And Taco Bell is right around the corner...

What to do? The worst thing you can do is give in to the temptation. It's going to cost you time as well as money. The second worst thing to do is suck it up and wait until you get home. For those of us who are really affected by low blood sugar, you might make mistakes in whatever you're doing or treat people with a little more curtness than is necessary. Perhaps worse, you might arrive back home cranky and foggy, and that's the last thing you want to be when you greet your loved ones (and have to unload groceries).

If you find yourself in these situations often, it's a good idea to keep a can of nuts or stash of granola bars in the car. You probably only need a snack to make it through, and you'll be proud of yourself for resisting the temptation to get fast food, making it even easier to do so next time.

As for those long car trips, when it's customary to stop for fast food, put extra snacks on your grocery list—the kind of snacks you look forward to eating, like BBQ chips and peanut M&Ms. Get ingredients for good sandwiches with all the fixings, such as pastrami or smoked turkey breast with provolone. Admit it: if you've packed a PB&J and told yourself you'll eat it for lunch after driving for hours, you're probably lying to yourself. When your stomach starts growling, you know you're going to take the off-ramp toward the golden arches.

You should be seeing a pattern by now: spend with purpose. To know what you're aiming for, you need to think ahead of time. It's the people who fly by the seat of their pants whose bank accounts are hemorrhaging cash.

Ok, you're not eating out. Now what?

Let's say you've successfully broken the cycle of eating out and you're buying groceries every week. What should you buy, and how much should you be spending on food? Answers in the FIRE community typically range from less than a $1 a meal to maybe $3. That might sound impossible, but if you buy in bulk and prepare your food yourself (no frozen enchiladas, Hot Pockets, or TV dinners), it's very doable. "Miscellaneous foods" and "bakery products" amount to $1,072 of the average annual food budget.[12]

---

[12] Alex Morrell and Skye Gould, "A close look at Americans' food budget shows an obvious place to save money", *Business Insider*, last modified

These are mostly prepared meals like the ones we just mentioned; cutting those out and buying more ingredients for home prep instead will reduce your bill drastically.

On average, we spend about $50 a week on groceries to feed the three of us and another $20 for beer/wine and non-grocery items. That amounts to just under $0.80 per person, per meal. Our daughter is a toddler as of this writing and so she doesn't eat a lot, but even between both adults, that's $1.20 per person. We readily admit that we do occasionally buy frozen burritos or pizzas for those really exhausting days when we're too tired to fix dinner. Having something quick on hand also helps fight the takeout temptation. We try to find a balance between convenience and cost.

That $1.20 per meal per person isn't our dinner average though. Breakfast usually consists of eggs and cheese, oatmeal, cereal, or waffles. Breakfast is by far our cheapest meal at $0.05-$0.30/meal. Lunch usually consists of sandwiches, peanut butter and cheese, occasional unhealthy things like top ramen or mac n cheese and for big-batch dinners, leftovers. These usually come in at $0.25-$0.75/meal.

That leaves $2-4 for dinner. While that may seem low, consider this: Frozen chicken breasts cost about $4 for two pounds, 16 homemade tortillas cost about $0.50, a can of kidney beans or black beans is about $0.50 and the cost of white rice is negligible. Throw in some cheese, sour cream, and if you're feeling fancy, some avocado, and you have eight meals for around $1/person. Add some refried beans and a small salad, and you're looking at about $1.54/person/meal. That's about the cost of a tiny burger from the value menu. Clearly, eating at home can drastically reduce your food bill.

February 17, 2017, http://www.businessinsider.com/americans-spending-food-bls-2017-2

Whether you buy everything bulk or hardly anything, it can't be understated: **eat your leftovers**. Some people throw out their leftovers because they've planned their meals too close together, or they've cooked enough for one and a half nights, or one and a quarter nights. They don't have enough to make what's left into another meal for every member of the household, and due to the amount of prepared foods they keep on hand for lunch (or they buy lunch everyday), the leftovers are passed over and eventually spoil in the fridge. Saving 33% by buying bulk won't do you much good if you're throwing out half your meals anyway.

If you do hit a snag with your meal plan and know you won't be able to eat the leftovers, consider freezing it. Most soups, chilis, and shredded cooked meats freeze pretty well. You can even freeze loaves of bread. *Save what you can.* One of those nights when you're too exhausted to even think about cooking something from scratch, you'll be thankful for that half lasagna in the freezer.

If you're in the habit of freezing leftovers and meats (that you probably bought multiples of because they were on sale), especially if they don't come in large, clearly labeled bags, *keep a spreadsheet of what you have in your freezer* so you know what you need to buy and what you already have. Keeping records (just like the recipe book) will reduce the effort it takes to come up with meals for the week. You don't need to dig through your fridge to find those pork chops you *think* you have or wing it and risk paying for something twice and letting the first item get freezer burned. You can just pull up your spreadsheet and see what you have. Better yet, print it out and put it on your freezer (as we do) so you know what you have without the need to go to your computer.

Sample Freezer Contents Table

Type	Weight	Date frozen
Pork chops	2.4 lbs.	1/26/18
Bacon	2.0 lbs.	1/26/18
Pork tenderloin	3.1. lbs.	1/26/18
Broccoli	5.0 lbs. bag	2/12/18
Cauliflower	~2.5 lbs. (half bag)	2/12/18
Lasagna	~4 servings	3/1/18
Rump roast (beef)	3.2 lbs.	3/24/18

The larger point here is that being organized saves you time, effort, stress, and money. Get efficient. Keep your pantry neat so you can easily check for ingredients. Planning meals may seem tedious on Saturday morning (or whatever time you designate for this), but it smooths your evenings out for the rest of week.

But won't I get tired of eating the same kinds of things?

One of the common beliefs among early retirees is that the same **staple foods** (chicken, beef, rice, beans, potatoes, pasta) **can be prepared over and over in different ways.** What brings variety and excitement to the dish is usually spices. So, if your spice cupboard is bare, stock up. Our household makes liberal use of cumin, paprika, garlic and onion powders, dill, cinnamon and red pepper flakes. Soy sauce, Worcestershire sauce, balsamic vinegar and hot sauce can also help jazz up our staple foods.

Useful Cooking Tools

A pressure cooker is a good investment if you don't have one. Pressure cookers allow you to do "slow food, fast," meaning your pork tenderloin will be ready after two hours and your chili can be done in half an hour. Beef stew is a winter favorite for the pressure cooker and has cheap ingredients like potatoes and carrots. Alternatively, you can make slow food, slow and get dinner started in the morning. It'll be ready for you when you finish work and your house will smell delicious. Chinese takeout just can't compare to a slow cooker Mississippi roast.

Believe it or not, that big bulky bread maker sitting on the bottom shelf is really easy to use and can save you even more money. Ours was passed on to us from Cody's parents, and we use it at least once a week to make a basic loaf of bread. On average, a homemade loaf of simple white or wheat bread will cost about $.53.[13] The cheapest loaf at the grocery store will cost at least twice that, and it won't taste *nearly* as good.

If that sounds like way too much effort for 50 cents a week, we get it. But if you have a bread maker, you at least owe it to yourself to give it a shot.

There are tons of resources out there to help you make the best decisions on where to buy your toilet paper and toothpaste and ground beef. Those prices will change and depend on what stores are in your area and where you're located, so it's of little use to hash out the minutia in this book. Our aim is that you take away four keys to successfully reigning in your food costs:

1) Break the habit of eating out
2) Develop a grocery shopping routine
3) Stay organized and keep inventory
4) Buy in bulk and multiples

The four points all rely on each other. It's easier to buy multiples on sale if you know you can eat the product before they spoil or get freezer-burned, which you can be confident of because you're tracking your inventory. Tracking your inventory makes it easier to

---

[13] Kristen, "Does homemade bread really save money?", *The Frugal Girl*, last modified August 25, 2010, http://www.thefrugalgirl.com/2010/08/wednesday-baking-does-homemade-bread-save-money/

write a grocery list, and easy grocery list-making makes it easier to stay in the routine of regular grocery shopping. Regular grocery shopping, in turn, will make eating out harder to justify and eating in more of a habit.

Through these methods, you should be able to put together a healthy, delicious meal plan that should add up to about $25/person/week. Add in some drinks and non-grocery items that you buy in bulk (toilet paper, toothpaste, deodorant) and you should be able to escape the grocery store with a bill of $35/person for the week or an annual expense of $1,820/person. As we'll detail in the true cost of raising kids, this amount gets even lower per person as you increase the size of your household.

With that said, let's get into some other cost reforms you can start working on right now.

Chapter 3

The Easy 3: Phone, Cable, and Internet

Besides reforming your spending on food, the easiest places to cut your monthly costs are your phone, cable, and internet bills.

Let's look at your phone costs first.

Phones

The average consumer spent close to a thousand dollars ($963) on their cell phone hardware and plans in 2014.[14] That's about $80 a month. This grows to $1,315 a year if you include a residential phone line.

But prices have dropped dramatically since then as more carriers have entered the market. Consumers have more competition over their business than ever before. If you're dropping 80 bucks a month on a single phone line, you're getting fleeced. A quick analysis of the best plans as reported by NerdWallet[15] shows the average cost of a good plan to be about $40 for 5GB of data or more (most Americans use more than five gigs a month).

What's really going to make the biggest cost difference for you is reducing your data usage. Do you really need five gigs a month?

---

[14] Brett Creech, "Expenditures on cellular phone services have increased significantly since 2007", *Bureau of Labor Statistics,* last modified February 3, 2016, https://www.bls.gov/opub/btn/volume-5/expenditures-on-celluar-phone-services-have-increased-significantly-since-2007.htm
[15] Kelsey Sheehy, "Best Cell Phone Plans", *nerdwallet,* last modified August 2, 2017, https://www.nerdwallet.com/blog/utilities/cell-phone-plans/

Probably not. The less time you spend on social media, the happier you'll be anyway. You can listen to a downloaded audiobook in the waiting room at the doctor's office or in the car instead. Your kids especially don't need five gigs of data and would probably benefit from have it severely restricted. Research from British psychologists found that young adults are on their phones nearly twice as much as they self-report—around five hours a day.[16] That's a *third* of waking hours staring at a smartphone.

You probably don't need five gigs, just like you don't need a lot of things that marketers and gurus tell us we need. And capping your data at one or two gigs will force you to be more conservative with your data usage. Besides, most places you need to be for long periods of time, like your home or office, have wifi.

We each have a Republic Wireless plan with 1GB of 4G LTE data for $20/month - about $25 after tax. As of this writing, Republic offers a $15/month plan for unlimited talk and text, and $5/month for every gig of data you add to the plan. We're paying nearly half of what "the best" plans are for the average consumer, according to NerdWallet.

So, would you get half the quality of the "better" network plans? It depends on where you live and where you travel to. You can check coverage in your area on the Republic Wireless website. The company is currently "hosted" by Sprint's network. As a "virtual operator," RW uses a combination of wifi hotspots, which your phone switches to automatically, and a normal cell network. Though it might sound like a clumsy budget patchwork, in our experience, it works pretty smoothly.

Now, about the hardware. As of this writing, the iPhone X retails at $999, and the iPhone 8 at $699. The Galaxy Note 8 costs $960. We got Moto G5 Plus's for $139.20 each, after utilizing a coupon. In less than a year, we'd recouped the cost of both phones, because the RW plan was so much cheaper than the average.

---

[16] Sally Andrews and David A. Ellis and Heather Shaw and Lukasz Piwek, "Beyond Self-Report: Tools to Compare Estimated and Real-World Smartphone Use", *PLOS,* last modified October 28, 2015, http://journals.plos.org/plosone/article?id=10.1371/journal.pone.013900 4

Perhaps you chafe at the suggestion to ditch your high-end phone. "I quite like my iPhone 8, thank you very much. I don't want to go through the trouble of learning a new phone and detangling myself from my carrier."

Small choice, big impact

Let's put this cost in perspective for the long-term to see if we can change your mind. We know that the best "value" plans are roughly $20 more than our $24.92 Republic Wireless plan. Let's assume your journey to FIRE takes ten years and you go with the more expensive plan. That $20 difference, if you invested it monthly over ten years at a 7% real return, ends up being about $3,500.[17] Additionally, after you hit FIRE, you'd need to sustain that additional $20 expense indefinitely. We'll go into depth on how much you need to retire in a later chapter, but the gist is that you need enough to have about 25x your annual spending (the rule of 25 or the "4% rule") in investments. That $240 additional annual expense would then mean you'd need to save an additional $6,000. Add it together, and the impact ends up being nearly $10,000.

But, let's say you're one of those that are paying around $80/month *and* you don't intend on retiring early. For this example, we'll assume you're 20. This means you'd pay more than $55/month than we do for the next 45 years. Once you turn 65, you also needed to have saved enough to cover that additional $55 expense until you kick the bucket. Using the rule of 25 discussed above, this equates to $16,500.

That's bad enough, but what if you had instead invested that extra $55/month for your 45-year working career? That $16,500 figure becomes $210,530.74![18] Add in the $16,500 and you're looking at a total impact of over $225,000.

---

[17] "Compound Interest Calculator" *U.S. Securities and Exchange Commission*, last modified August 25, 2016, https://www.investor.gov/additional-resources/free-financial-planning-tools/compound-interest-calculator

[18] "Compound Interest Calculator" *U.S. Securities and Exchange Commission*, last modified August 25, 2016,

The question is this: Does your iPhone X bring about enough satisfaction to justify an extra five years of work? Based on the average salary in 2017,[19] that's the sort of damage you're looking at with a recurring expense of a pricey cell phone plan.

Let that sink in for a moment. That's the cost of a pretty nice house in many suburban areas.

What we're getting at is that this kind of money is worth a couple hours' trouble, and even the early termination fee that might hit you if you break your contract.

Cable and Satellite

With the growing popularity and variety included in streaming services, millions of people have already "cut the cord." You should consider doing the same. According to a survey of 3,013 respondents in the U.S. and Canada, 64.7% report they pay between $51 and $125 for cable or satellite per month.[20] Comparatively, Netflix's middle tier plan costs $10.99. Even their best plan, which allows 4K streaming on up to four devices, costs $13.99. Hulu costs $7.99 a month, and Amazon Prime, which gets you free two-day shipping on millions of online purchases, includes a robust streaming service with original content for $99 a year. All three of these services would cost about $30 a month. Yet some people are paying more for their cable plans than the annual cost of any one of these services *monthly*.

To put these costs in perspective, Prime, Hulu, and Netflix would cost $362.76 a year. A lower end cable bill of $60 would cost you

---

https://www.investor.gov/additional-resources/free-financial-planning-tools/compound-interest-calculator

[19] "Table 3. Median usual weekly earnings of full-time wage and salary workers by age, race, Hispanic or Latino ethnicity, and sex, fourth quarter 2017 averages, not seasonally adjusted", *Bureau of Labor Statistics,* last modified January 17 2018, https://www.bls.gov/news.release/wkyeng.t03.htm

[20] "How much is your monthly cable/satellite bill for TV services?", *Statista*, last modified 2017, https://www.statista.com/statistics/793014/monthly-cable-satellite-bill/

nearly twice that at $720, meaning you'll pay an extra $29.77 every month for a basic cable plan over a suite of streaming services. Assuming your journey to FIRE takes ten years, this equates to $5,172.92.[21] You'll also need to save enough money to cover the cost of cable during retirement (assuming you don't want to deflate your lifestyle in retirement). That's $8,931, using the 4% rule.

Do you want to work nearly an extra 3-4 months (assuming you're making the median salary of $44,564[22]) to cover the cost of cable? Maybe, but we don't.

Now, if you're a diehard sports fan, you might want to consider a middle ground option and just get cable for the months of the year your favorite sports are in season. For three years, we had cable for six months out of the year so we could watch football; the other six months, we suspended it (some cable providers have a "pause" option that temporarily deactivates your services until you're ready to use them again at a cost of just a few dollars for each month you're not using the service). You may want to investigate whether this is an option for you.

Internet

"Unbundling" can save you money. Bundling internet, home phone, and cable might be a good deal if you really use all three, but if not, you're probably not getting a good value. The number of households with landlines or VOIP for home phones has plummeted in recent years, primarily because everyone has a cell

---

[21] "Compound Interest Calculator" *U.S. Securities and Exchange Commission*, last modified August 25, 2016, https://www.investor.gov/additional-resources/free-financial-planning-tools/compound-interest-calculator

[22] "Table 3. Median usual weekly earnings of full-time wage and salary workers by age, race, Hispanic or Latino ethnicity, and sex, fourth quarter 2017 averages, not seasonally adjusted", *Bureau of Labor Statistics,* last modified January 17 2018, https://www.bls.gov/news.release/wkyeng.t03.htm

phone.[23] So if you have a home phone, consider ditching it. Then, if you really *really* think cable is worth it, you can find the best cable deal and the best internet deal. Check to see if there are independent ISPs (internet service providers) in your area who might be able to undercut the bigger competitors.

This requires research and perhaps several phone calls. Start by finding out how fast you really need your internet to be (you can use an online free meter to find out how fast it is currently) and how much data you need. Then, shop around and compare services.

Negotiate

Clear a few hours of your afternoon to make calls for reducing or eliminating the cost of each of these services. You probably already know that the first thing you should tell your current provider is that you're switching to (candidate 1) so you can get a better deal. They'll try to retain you; be patient, but firm. If they offer you what *sounds* like a better deal, interrogate them. What's the monthly estimate with taxes and fees? Will the quality of your service remain the same? Will you be locked into a new contract, and if so, what is their early termination fee? If their offer still checks out, fish that offer to candidate 1 to see if they can beat it. Eventually, one will stand out as the winner.

If you have the cash, you can also try to get a discount by prepaying for a year, as we did for our internet. After locking in the best rates you can find, set reminders to shop once a year to make sure you're always getting the best rates possible.

And if you were promised something you didn't end up getting, make a fuss. Businesses should keep their word, but it's up to you

---

[23] Stephen J Blumberg and Julian V. Luke, "Wireless Substitutions: Early Release of Estimates from the National Health Interview Survey, July-December 2016", *National Center for Health Statistics*, last modified May 4, 2017, https://www.cdc.gov/nchs/data/nhis/earlyrelease/wireless201705.pdf

to hold them to it. Politely but firmly escalate your issue up the chain of command until it is resolved to your satisfaction. When you're offered promises, get it in writing. Several major companies don't record phone calls and don't send email confirmations of the rates you were promised. When you find out your bill is more than you agreed to, you may be told, "We'd never offer a rate that low," and without proof, you'd have to pay the higher fee. While your initial contract may hold them to your original rate, promos and temporary credits you're promised over the phone need to be followed with a written confirmation.

But whether you're trying to resolve a problem or considering making a switch, be sure you're fed, well rested and free from distractions during the process, as negotiations can get frustrating.

You'd be shocked how much money you can save with a little time on the phone. We once reduced our bill for our quartz countertops by $400 because Cody noticed they had used more square feet than they needed to make the proper cuts. We also received steep discounts after escalating a pricing issue with our major cable provider to the office of the CEO. Though each of these issues were frustrating and took a couple hours of phone calls, if you look at your savings as an hourly wage of your phone call, the effort is well worth it. Through these methods, you can receive substantial savings on your phone, internet, and cable bills, and you can put the difference toward paying off debt or growing your nest egg.

On your quest to reduce your annual expenses, try to keep your internet bill to $50/month, your cell phone bill to $25/person/month and if possible, eliminate your cable bill. You can replace it with streaming services at $30/month which will likely still offer your favorite shows. We call these three—phones, cable, and internet— "the easy 3," as they can be dramatically reduced with relatively little effort. A few hours of phone calls can potentially shave hundreds of dollars off your monthly expenses, leaving you with a line item of about $100/month for all three services (plus $25 per additional person in your household that needs a cell phone).

Chapter 4

Getting Your Money's Worth in Entertainment

In the previous chapter, we discussed ways to lower your phone, cable, and internet bills. But if you're partial to spending nights out on the town drinking in bars, going to the movies, shopping, and eating out, you're probably spending more than you would on a robust collection of TV channels and streaming services.

For example, if you're married, you probably have a date night budget. We used to set aside $100 every month for date nights, but since the birth of our daughter, date nights are few and far between. When we do have a date, it's quite important we get our money's worth out of it. We've come to realize that cooking at home with fancy ingredients or ordering pizza and playing a board game is more fun than going out to a movie and a nice restaurant. At the end of the night, we go back to pick up our daughter from Grandma and Grandpa's house. We spend a fraction of what we would have spent on the traditional dinner and a movie, and we do it in the comfort of our own home.

Home Dinner Parties vs. Eating Out

That's not to say you should become a hermit. You need to be with other people on the regular, even more so if you're extroverted. But *going out* with friends isn't necessary for enjoying their company; it's simply habitual and cultural. The cost of hosting a small potluck and playing a board game, or simply sipping wine in the living room and having a conversation, is much lower. By dividing the cost of dinner among yourselves, you've drastically lowered the price by pooling your labor to prepare it. Just the fact that you don't have to pay a tip knocks 20% off the night's bill, and alcoholic beverages will cost about a quarter or less of what a restaurant would charge. Plus, at least one of you doesn't have to drive anywhere.

Let's say you all went to a diner and each of you ordered a burger costing on average $13. You each order a drink, costing $7. Now, each of you are paying $20 before tax and tip. Let's say tax is 8% and tip is 18%. Now you've each shelled out over $25. If you're a couple, that's a $50 hit to your household budget for a single meal. That's not including gas or childcare, which, if you don't live close to family, would be another $20 at least.

Now, let's say you still wanted burgers with your friends, but you want to do it at home. You have one couple bring beer and sides, another dessert and buns, and you supply the burgers. Beef can be had at $3.50/lb. and you'll need a couple pounds. Add in some swiss, mushrooms and onions and you're up to $10.00. You use a few other ingredients in your preparation, plus electricity or propane, which bumps the cost up by a dollar. Now you're out 11 bucks, but you're hosting, so you don't spend a dime on gas.

As a bonus (though perhaps some wouldn't consider it a bonus), you don't have to pay for childcare. Neither do your friends. We mention this because if one's children are well-behaved and can play well with others, they don't have to be unloaded onto a babysitter whenever mom or dad can't devote their full attention to parenting. Social time with friends can be doable even with kids around, especially if you have a house or yard with space enough for kids to be active. This can relieve pressure for you and your friends and free up opportunities to get together, since no one needs to arrange ahead of time for someone to take care of the kids.

During the spring and summer, you might also pack a potluck picnic and bring all the kids to the park to play. You can relax in the nice weather and chat, maybe play a game of frisbee or croquet, and the kids get screen-free play time outside. For *free*.

The Crazy ROI of Games and Books

Games are one of the most cost-effective ways to pass leisure time because you only need to purchase a board game once. If it costs $40, and you get a *mere* four hours of entertainment out of it, that's twice as much entertainment for the cost of a few movie tickets. We've probably spent at least 20 hours playing Splendor over the past year. Even if you aren't a game enthusiast, odds are overwhelmingly favorable that it will pay for itself. It might be hard to get friends or family interested in a board game or yard game, especially if it's one they haven't played. But time and again, our family has found that if you can get people to invest the initial ten minutes to learn a game, they tend to really enjoy themselves—and friends will probably ask to play that game again the next time they're over.

Video games can be a great entertainment investment, as well, in terms of hours of play per dollar spent. If you drop $60 on a new game and play 60 hours (which is *easy* to do), that's about as good of a return on investment as you can get. Playing online with friends can even be a sort of social activity, and it can build teamwork. The downside to gaming is its addictive nature,[24] and it's no joke. If you've been sucked into games in the past to the detriment of the rest of your life, it's probably best to keep your console in the closet.

You might be asking what makes games better than the infinite amount of entertainment you can find for free online via social media or YouTube. Well, in general you get what you pay for. To put it bluntly: do you want your brain to rot? Because that's what watching random videos of people falling off skateboards will do to you.

There are certainly many well-produced YouTube channels and interesting sites that enrich instead of rot your brain. But libraries

---

[24] Jane Wakefield, "Gaming addiction classified as disorder by WHO", *BBC News*, last modified January 2, 2018, http://www.bbc.com/news/technology-42541404

still have them beat. Without the distractions that come with simply being on the internet, the content of libraries tends to fortify your brain instead of rot it. You can get a lot more out than what you pay in with your tax dollars, and you don't even have to leave your home to do it. Many books can be downloaded from your library's website or from Hoopla, which is like a super-library (you must have a library card to access its content). Thousands of classic books are available as eBooks or audiobooks.

As it turns out, the more you read, the more you'll want to read. Reading can increase your knowledge and enrich your life with very little effort. If you instill a love of reading in your children, all the better: you're setting them up for success academically and beyond, not least because it diverts their attention away from digital games and video—and the evidence digital media is bad for kids' mental and physical development keeps growing.[25]

Make Home Entertainment the More Attractive Option

As far as entertainment for adults goes, you might not need time "away" from your kids as much as you need time *with* friends and extended family. What you need time away from might just be the day to day grind.

That brings us to an important question: If you are in the habit of going out during your "leisure" time, think about why that is. Is there something about being home that bothers you? Is it boring, cluttered, and dirty? Or maybe it's your relationship with members of your family; perhaps you don't want to spend any more time with them than you need to? Whatever the case may be, identify what's driving you to spend so much leisure time away from home.

All the practical tips in the world won't fix a problem that can only be identified and addressed by *you*, especially if the problems are

---

[25] May Bulman, "Children facing 'significant emotional risk' on social media, report warns", *Independent,* last modified January 4, 2018, http://www.independent.co.uk/news/uk/home-news/facebook-children-risk-emotional-impact-report-warning-a8140526.html

interpersonal. Many people make a habit of going out to bars in the evening because they have financial or marital troubles they want to forget about, or their kids are ill-behaved and drive them up the wall. Others go to "retail therapy" to forget their troubles and spend their time shopping for a quick (but not cheap) endorphin hit.

There's nothing inherently wrong with getting away every so often, either by yourself or with friends. But if it is a crutch you frequently employ to avoid addressing the real problems in your life, you need to recognize that and attempt to pull up the root of the issue. Avoiding your problems will only put you deeper in the financial and emotional pit.

Of course, it might not be a "problem" so much as a challenge. An outdated home, for instance. When we first moved into our house, it hadn't been updated in its 25 years of existence; the carpets that ran throughout the whole house were a boring taupe color, the cabinets were a displeasing honey oak color typical of the 90s, and every single wall was white. We loved our house from the outside, but on the inside, we couldn't wait to at least paint the walls. For certain personalities especially, a dreary environment can't keep you any longer than absolutely necessary.

So, see what you can do with your budget to liven up your environment. A coat of paint, some throw pillows, or new curtains can make your space more inviting with minimal costs. Don't worry about what other people might think when they visit your home. Think about the kinds of space *you* like to be in. If it makes your home more comfortable, you'll probably get your money back in the form of lesser entertainment expenditures.

Not least among the things that can drive you out of your own home is messiness. If you neglect your home, where you likely spend over half your life, you're setting yourself up for failure. Not just financially, but emotionally and mentally. Be diligent. Clean something every day: the carpets, the coffee table, the toilets. Just *something* beyond the bare minimum of picking up the Legos.

Consider setting up a chore chart; if your kids are old enough for chores, they certainly should be pulling their weight. They make most of the messes, after all.

It's true that a house with small children is in a constant state of entropy, but you can maintain some level of order. Have a large toy bin readily accessible to throw toys into. Put toys your kid has outgrown away in the closet to reduce the clutter or give them away. Clean out your "junk" drawer regularly. Organize your pantry when you have a spare ten minutes. All these things, when they become habit, make your home more habitable and enjoyable to be in. If you can put money toward minor to moderate renovations, all the better. You'll probably get most of that money back when you sell, and you can enjoy it in the meantime.

Think about it this way: your home is likely your biggest monthly expenditure; shouldn't you be getting your money's worth? Make your home a space you want to live in, and you'll be happy to relax in it and share it with friends. Saving money might just be a secondary benefit.

So how much should entertainment cost you? Although it's hard to set a budget for entertainment because of how much it encompasses, we say about $75/month for a couple should suffice. This should cover date nights, time with friends, movies and games. If you have kids, add another $40/month per child starting at age 5 in the form of an allowance they can use for both learning the fundamentals of savings and for the occasional game, activity, or candy bar.

Chapter 5

Getting Around Comfortably and Cheaply

While some city dwellers might be content to live a car-free life, the automobile is still emblematic of American prosperity, freedom and independence. Whether you like having a car or not, for people living outside the urban cores, a vehicle is likely a necessity—if not now, then at some point in the future.

Now, it's one thing to own a car, it's another to *finance* a car. Unfortunately, most Americans don't see a distinction between the two. One of America's worst financial habits is financing cars. Like getting a mortgage, it's just something you *do* as long as you qualify for the monthly payments. We, too, fell for this cultural trap. Having a car payment on top of student loans didn't exactly set us up for financial success, especially that early in life—and neither will it for you.

The Budget Crusher: A Car Payment

The Bureau of Labor Statistics reports that $3,634 of the average annual household budget goes to "new vehicle purchases."[26] But the BLS category of "new vehicle purchases" doesn't even contain spending on car payments—that goes in the "other vehicle expenses" category ($2,884), along with maintenance and insurance costs. Altogether, that's roughly $240 a month, but

---

[26] "Consumer spending on vehicles averaged $8,427 in 2016", *Bureau of Labor Statistics,* last modified September 11, 2017, https://stats.bls.gov/opub/ted/2017/consumer-spending-on-vehicles-averaged-8427-in-2016.htm

that's an average of individuals with and *without* car payments. The cost is much higher for people who've financed their vehicles. In 2015, the average used car loan was $361 a month, according to data from Experian.[27] For new cars, it was $483.

But wait! It gets worse. If you have bad credit, you might be in the "subprime" or "deep subprime" (yes, that's a real term, but "deep sh*t" seems more appropriate) category so many sleazy car dealerships prey upon. For you, it could be $512 a month. That's over $6,000 a year. A *year*. You could buy a pretty solid vehicle *in cash* for $6,000, throw it away every year, buy a new one, rinse and repeat, and still be better off.

Regardless of the exact payments, do you really want to be waist deep in debt *of any kind* for the rest of your life? If you plan on achieving and sustaining FIRE, the answer should be no. Those monthly payments necessitate such a high investment number to be sustained that it can make your FIRE number unachievable. Consider a $450 car payment you plan to keep your entire life (through trade-ins that extend your loan term indefinitely). Using the rule of 25, you'd need to save $135,000 to safely sustain that payment. How long would it take you to save this much money? Is it really worth having a car with a few extra inches of storage space, a few new gadgets and luxuries and marginally better gas mileage?

Next to credit card debt (barring extreme emergencies), car debt is the least necessary sort of debt. Yet it's ubiquitous. That's owing not just to constant marketing by car companies, but the common misconceptions people have about cars.

For instance, people seem to be under the impression that newer cars are significantly safer than older cars (we're talking 5-15 years old), but by and large, that's not the case. It's true that manufacturers started using stronger steel for frames in the early

---

[27] Melinda Zabritski, "State of the Automotive Finance Market Second Quarter 2015", *Experian Automotive,* last modified 2015, https://www.experian.com/assets/automotive/white-papers/experian-auto-2015-q2.pdf?WT.srch=Auto_Q12015FinanceTrends_PDF

2000s[28] and that helps protect occupants in severe crashes, but all cars in this range have ABS and airbags, which are the most critical safety features. Lane-assist and backup cameras are appealing, but they're merely aids in doing what drivers should already be doing: paying attention.

Then there's the prevailing notion that a new car will virtually guarantee reliability. Even if this were true, is it worth paying an arm, leg, and firstborn child for a "guarantee" it won't break down for the first 60,000 miles that you own it? What if instead you had no car payment, and set aside a little every month in case your older car does break down (and you can be pleasantly surprised when year after year, your car muscles through without a major issue)? Is your life so incredibly important that you couldn't bear it if you had to miss work for a day or take a bus while your car is in the shop? Will life as you know it *end?*

We know how irritating it can be to own a lemon. Cody's second car, a 2002 Ford Escape, was a lemon. We were so desperate to unload it and so irritated by its fickleness, we traded it in for a new, fully-loaded 2012 Honda Civic. And yes, we had *that* size car payment—$465, to be precise. We've been on the worst side of "owning" a new car and owning an older car.

The Gut-Punch of Lost Value

As always, being smart with your money means being a discerning consumer. You have to do your research to avoid getting suckered. There are loads of resources that can tell you which older models you should avoid and which ones will be worth every dollar, but what many summaries of car pros and cons won't tell you is how well a car holds its value. You must look not just at safety, reliability, and gas mileage, but how much value the car will lose while you own it. Financially speaking, that's a big deal.

---

[28] Mike Mueller, "Timeline: A Path to Lightweight Materials in Cars and Trucks", *Office of Energy Efficiency & Renewable Energy,* last modified August 25, 2016, https://energy.gov/eere/articles/timeline-path-lightweight-materials-cars-and-trucks

A new car loses about 9% of its value when you drive it off the lot.[29] Five years later, it's lost 60% of its initial value. Do you want to be the sucker that pays a small fortune every month to drive a "new" car, and then when you trade it in, it's worth less than the balance of your loan? And then you start the process *all over again?*

If you're financing a used car older than five years, it won't depreciate nearly as fast. But depending on how old it is, you could still get suckered. Here's a good rule of thumb: *if it costs enough that you can't buy it in cash, you can't afford it.*

Getting past "everybody does it"

This is one of those instances where if you want to take charge of your financial situation, you need to be countercultural. Spending less on groceries and eating out is something pretty much everyone is trying to do, to varying degrees of success. But ditching a car payment in favor of an older vehicle bought in cash—that's a relatively conspicuous life choice. The roads are full of older vehicles, of course, so you won't be as conspicuous on the road. But a downgrade is still obvious socially; it will raise a few eyebrows among your friends. Worse, it will *feel* like a downgrade. And it will probably feel like you're depriving yourself of a luxury you've earned by hard work.

When we came to our senses and traded in our Honda Civic, it did feel a little like that. Our "new" 2000 Nissan Altima had about 150,000 miles on it, which we paid for with $2,400 in cash. It had some obvious scratches, the casing for the power seat controls on the driver's side had come loose, and the serpentine belt squealed like a banshee when we turned the air conditioner on at times. But it was clean and well-maintained on the inside and it ran well. We missed the Bluetooth stereo and the heated seats of the Civic, but

---

[29] "Depreciation Infographic: How Fast Does My New Car Lose Value?", *Edmunds,* last modified September 24, 2010, https://www.edmunds.com/car-buying/how-fast-does-my-new-car-lose-value-infographic.html

after a month or so, we adjusted. It was well worth it for the relief of not having a car payment.

We also ended up self-installing our own Bluetooth stereo with $100 and the help of a Youtube video. As it turns out, the Altima is nearly as comfortable and has more horsepower. It got us where we needed to go and didn't break down in the four years we owned it. It's the exact opposite of the lemon experience we had with the Ford Explorer, which appeared to have no superficial blemishes but was rotting away on the inside.

So, do your research. Not all older cars are of equal quality, so they don't hold their value equally either. But even if you shell out $2,400 on a troublemaker, you'll lose a lot less money over financing that brand new car. Not to mention, the cost of insuring an older vehicle is far less, as your ability to replace a totaled older car out of pocket allows you to go with liability coverage as opposed to full coverage. Our Civic's full coverage cost $95 a month. Our Altima's liability coverage costs $25.

After admonishing you to please, please not finance a vehicle...we must add a caveat. And it's only for people who are extremely fastidious with their dollars and for some reason accept the premise that they need a car nice enough to demand a higher price tag ($10,000+). Perhaps you hold a job that necessitates a certain image.

If you can get a very low interest rate on financing the vehicle, and if you have the cash in hand to pay for it outright, then you could keep your dollars and invest them in the market instead of sinking them all at once into a depreciating asset. Your dollars *could* (and likely will) "work harder" for you (again, we'll discuss historical returns in a later chapter) than if you put them all towards a vehicle at once.

However, we recommend getting a vehicle with a net cost of no more than $6,000 after you've sold or traded in your previous vehicle. At that price point, your market returns, even if they're a few percentage points above the car loan interest rate, would create such a small difference that you'd be better off just buying the car with cash.

What about the other Transportation Costs?

Americans spent roughly $9,000 on transportation costs in 2016.[30] That's almost 16% of the average household budget of approximately $57,000, according to the Bureau of Labor Statistics.[31]

The biggest recurring transportation expense for car owners besides the monthly payments is gas. Nearly two grand ($1,909) is spent on gas and oil. By comparison, we spend about $60 a month on gas and $10-$15 every six months to change the oil and filter (which we usually do ourselves). That comes to about $750 a year or about 40% of what the average person spends on gas and oil.

What gives? It's not like we're driving a Prius with a crazy high MPG. We get about 23 miles to the gallon in the city.

Well, one of us works from home, and the other works outside the home only twice a week, at a job only a few miles away from our house. We attend church once a week, grocery shop once a week, and visit family once a week—all those places are 5-15 minutes away. Every other month, we drive four hours to visit family out of town, and we go out maybe once a week for an errand, but all in all, we just don't drive a lot.

---

[30] "Consumer spending on vehicles averaged $8,427 in 2016", *Bureau of Labor Statistics,* last modified September 11, 2017, https://stats.bls.gov/opub/ted/2017/consumer-spending-on-vehicles-averaged-8427-in-2016.htm
[31] "Consumer Expenditures--2016", *Bureau of Labor Statistics,* last modified August 29, 2017, https://www.bls.gov/news.release/cesan.nr0.htm

You know where we're going with this. The best thing you can do for your transportation budget is to decrease your car commute. There are a few ways you can do this:

1. Work from home

If you've only just entered the workforce, this probably isn't an option for you. But if you're a valued employee in an office job, you might be able to negotiate a work from home situation. If you can't swing a full time WFH gig, even web-commuting once or twice a week can help cut costs.

2. Find work closer to home

The upside to being a young entry-level employee is the possibility of finding a similar job (barista, server, bank teller, cashier, etc.) closer to where you live, as those positions are common and fairly generic. Even those of you further along in your careers can keep an eye out for WFH positions or jobs with shorter commutes.

3. Ride a bike or take public transportation

We walked to work for several months when we first started our journey to FIRE. It was about a 20-minute walk, and we're not going to lie: it was miserable in the rain. But on the upside, we were more alert when we got to work, we got daily exercise, and gained a new appreciation for the dry, warm comfort of car travel.

4. Carpool

If you live on a colleague's route to work, or vice versa, consider pooling resources so you can split the cost of gas. You might also be able to avoid or reduce the cost of heavy tolls by using the carpool lane.

5. Find a home closer to work

If you're leasing an apartment, finding a unit closer to work could be fairly easy. But for home owners, this is the most difficult of the options and the hardest to justify. Jobs are often less permanent and more easily replaceable than your house, especially if you've made a lot of memories there. If you already plan on moving, however, proximity to work should be a top priority when choosing a new house or apartment.

You've probably seen those HGTV shows where the late twenty-something couple says, "I know we wanted a house close to Erin's job, but this place out in the sticks just has so much character!" Don't be that couple. A long commute is one of the surest ways to decrease your quality of life,[32] next to a poor diet and a lack of exercise. It increases anxiety, decreases time spent with family and friends, decreases time available for sleeping and housework, and the trip itself consistently oscillates between boring and frustrating. Honestly, the expense might be the least terrible thing about long commutes.

So even if a house far from work is your *dream* house except for its distance from work, *don't buy it*. Don't even think about it. The open floor plan and cute breakfast nook are not going to make up for the stress and cost of commuting. It is better to live in a humble home with happy people than a luxurious one with cranky commuters.

But since we're mostly concerned with the cost here, consider the results of investing that $1,189 (the difference between our $720 annual transportation cost and the average $1,909). In ten years, you'd have approximately $17,401.89.[33] Add in the $29,725 (using the 4% rule) you'd save by not needing to sustain that increased expense post-FIRE, and you're looking at a total impact of

---

[32] Carolyn Kylstra, "10 Things Your Commute Does to Your Body", *Time*, last modified February 26, 2014, http://time.com/9912/10-things-your-commute-does-to-your-body/

[33] "Compound Interest Calculator" *U.S. Securities and Exchange Commission*, last modified August 25, 2016, https://www.investor.gov/additional-resources/free-financial-planning-tools/compound-interest-calculator

$47,126.89. Not only is your commute killing your health, it's making you work for an additional year!

You may have a car loan now and you may even be underwater on your loan (that is, you owe more than what it's worth), but don't be discouraged. We were in the same situation and lost $10,000 on our financed Civic when we sold it. Just keep putting money towards principal until your loan balance equals the value of the car (if you're already there, great!) and save up enough money to where you can buy a used car ($2,000-$6,000) in cash. Once you've reached both milestones, sell your car and buy your used replacement.

Once you do this, push for liability insurance in the $20-$40 range and try to get your fuel bill down to $50-80/month. To keep your budget consistent, set aside $50/month for a "car maintenance or replacement fund." A $6,000 car should last you at least 12 years, and setting aside $50/month over this time span will generate the $6,000 you'll eventually need to replace it, along with occasional repairs. If you invest this money over ten years, it will likely grow beyond your base $7,200 in contributions, but keep in mind that this comes with some risks (e.g. the market crashing shortly before you pull the funds to make your purchase).

We understand some of you might be in a situation where you can't shorten your commute and that $100 line item in your budget for both gas and insurance just isn't feasible. If so, you'll need to make some cuts elsewhere. Even if this applies to you, getting your expenses down to $20,000/year if you're single or $30,000/year if your married is still doable. We'll take a look at another major expense you could save on in the next chapter.

Chapter 6

The Big One: Your Home

Regardless of whether you're currently renting or owning, your house, apartment, or condo is likely your biggest expense each month. Up to this point, we've covered expenses that are relatively easy to reduce or eliminate. Want to cut cable? A few calls will do it. Want to reduce your grocery bill? A little discipline and planning will get you there.

Well if you want to reduce your rent payment or mortgage payment, a lot more work is required.

Buying a home is traditionally considered part of the "American dream," though some early retirees argue it's a bad investment and that renting is the way to go. JL Collins, author of *The Simple Path to Wealth* and renowned in the FIRE space, penned a blog post in 2013 called, "Why Your House is a Terrible Investment."[34] He makes some strong points: houses are immobile, can depreciate, require maintenance costs, are complicated to buy and sell and are heavily taxed (every single year, not just when it's bought and sold).

When you settle into a house, you're also at the mercy of your neighbors. Not just the everyday stuff like having their trash blow into your yard or hearing their dogs bark at night (which you might also deal with if you rent a house), but if they're "motivated" to sell,

---

[34] JL Collins, "Why your house is a terrible investment", *jlcollinsnh*, last modified May 29, 2013, http://jlcollinsnh.com/2013/05/29/why-your-house-is-a-terrible-investment/

it can "set the price for the whole neighborhood," meaning you might take a loss if you're selling around the same time.

The housing market is also prone to bubbles, especially since the federal government loves to meddle in this issue by providing generous SALT (state and local tax) deductions, mortgage interest deductions, and occasionally encouraging subprime lending. Prices rise to ridiculous heights, and then when people realize a bunch of people own houses who can't be counted on to pay their mortgages (like what happened in '08), prices plummet. If you bought anywhere near the top of the market, you might have been underwater on your mortgage.

So, should you rent?

We argue that you should buy, unless you're in a market that heavily favors renting. For example, we found a 1,457 square foot house with two bedrooms and one bathroom for rent in Spokane, WA for $1,150 a month. By comparison, we found a 1,676 square foot house in the same neighborhood, also with two bedrooms and one bathroom, for $165,000. Using a mortgage calculator[35] that projects property tax, insurance *and* PMI on the 0% down payment (we're using a 0% down payment here to create an apples-to-apples comparison), the monthly mortgage payment on this house would be around $1,050. If you add in maintenance/repairs, the cost ends up being roughly equivalent for renting versus owning, which is standard with most low cost of living areas. Of course, the benefit to buying in this situation is that 15-30 years later, the buyer will have paid off his mortgage. This also goes to show that the costs of home ownership are built into your rent payment.

But what about a high cost of living metropolitan area like Seattle? We found a 1,435 square foot townhouse in Ballard for rent with 3 bedrooms and 2.5 baths for $2,900/month. By comparison, we found the same townhouse next door with the exact same specs for

---

[35] "U.S. Mortgage Calculator with Taxes, Insurance and PMI", last modified May 2, 2017, https://usmortgagecalculator.org/

$747,000. Using a mortgage calculator with the same assumptions as above, the monthly mortgage payment on this house comes out to around *$4,585*! As you can see, buying in some markets doesn't make sense over renting.

You'll want to run the numbers yourself, based on the area you live in. We've found PMI (Private Mortgage Insurance - a fee that covers the risk for those who don't have 20% saved for a down payment) on a loan to be around 0.75% of the loan amount per year. Property taxes can typically be found on Zillow. Interest rates are usually around 4% and home insurance is often about 0.35% of the property value. We recommend using these parameters with an online calculator, like usmortgagecalculator.org, to find out how much more or less a mortgage payment would cost over the equivalent home's rent payment.

If it is less than 20% more than the equivalent rent payment, buying makes more sense than renting if you plan on being in that area for at least five years. Why? Because although there are definitive drawbacks to home ownership as JL Collins points out, you'll eventually pay that mortgage off. Though the average homeowner hops from mortgage to mortgage his entire life, *you* are not average. You're going to eventually pay off a mortgage. And once that happens, your expenses will drop dramatically. But if you rent, you'll be making that rent payment forever.

Additionally, as we'll detail in Chapter 16, owning a home as opposed to renting will allow you to decrease the amount you'll need for retirement, getting you to FIRE much faster.

With that said, there are some things to keep in mind if you do choose to buy:

1)   Rent proponents argue that people who buy typically buy for the future. Maybe a 2-bedroom, 1-bath apartment works for you now, but you'll have kids in five years and that won't work then. So, shouldn't you buy a house with four bedrooms now, in preparation for the future? If you do, then you may have been better off

renting. In situations like this, it's better to wait to buy until you're ready to have kids. Although your rent payment isn't paying off any principal and it may feel like you're flushing money down the toilet each month, keeping your smaller apartment and saving $1,000 on what the increased monthly mortgage for a larger home would have been will represent a larger savings than what your principal payment would have provided.

2)   Rent proponents also argue that the down payment you'll likely need for your home would've been better off invested elsewhere. While this point holds validity, there are several loan programs available that allow you to buy a home with little-to-no down. Some have PMI that penalize doing this, but some programs, like those from the VA and USDA, will allow you to purchase a home with little to no down and no PMI (although some of these programs charge a set annual fee). Even if you do end up putting 20% down, you'll guarantee a positive return of whatever your interest rate is, and it gets you that much closer to paying off the mortgage completely, thus reducing your annual expenses and the amount you need for retirement.

3)   Your fixed mortgage payment can hurt more during times of deflation. Your $1,200 mortgage payment may look good now, when renting the same home costs $1,500. But if deflation comes in and reduces rental costs for a similar home to $1,000/month, your mortgage payment may start to look a lot more expensive. Homes do tend to appreciate, however, and typically your fixed mortgage payment will look more favorable as time goes on.

We understand not everyone will be able to buy. Perhaps you live in a high-cost-of-living area, or maybe you don't have enough money for a down payment on a house. Perhaps you don't have good enough credit to qualify for a mortgage or maybe you want to be more flexible with where you live and fear that purchasing a home will tie you down to that area. These are all valid concerns.

Even if you have enough for a down payment for a mortgage and the credit required, it might not be the right time. If you've just come out of college, you probably have a pile of student loans you need to pay off before you can think about buying a house. And the more earning capacity you can open yourself up to by staying mobile, the better the odds you can pay off your debt faster. You might even decide on going car-less to reduce your transportation costs and because of this, need to live close to work. If the neighborhood close to work has insane house prices, then renting is a pretty rational choice.

The priceless side of deciding where to live

We've made some practical points on owning vs. renting. But we're not robots making cold hard calculations to maximize earnings and savings. We're humans and we understand there's a high emotional element attached to home ownership. As we mentioned before, owning a home is considered part of the American Dream. It's not because it's always the superior financial decision. It's because a home is, for most intents and purposes, *yours*. You can paint it, refloor it, add to it, landscape the property, add amenities...you can do mostly whatever you want, bureaucratic meddling notwithstanding. You can make it your *home*, not just a temporary residence. In a rental, you're lucky if they let you paint a single wall.

The fact that homeowners are "tied down" can, in a sense, be a good thing. Arguably, Americans move too much. Nuclear families who move a lot find can find plugging into local communities a challenge. It's hard to put down roots when you're used to moving every few years, especially if you don't belong to a local church or some other sort of social organization.

Before we moved into our first (and current) house, we moved to a different apartment every year. We moved four times within the same city, an hour from extended family in one direction and three hours in the other. Even though Cody worked for the same company for most of that time, we felt isolated. You can isolate yourself in any situation, of course, but it happens to be much easier if you keep hopping around.

It's not just a sense of independence and the opportunity to build a social network that home ownership offers, though. As a property owner, you also have a stake in the wellbeing of the community. You want to see it succeed. When the local economy is strong, your home is worth more, you have more opportunities for work, more choices for necessities, and more options for leisure. You're more keenly aware of the rates at which you're taxed, and the efficacy with which those tax dollars are spent. You want to see your neighbors take care of their properties, for the crime rate to decline, and for the quality of the schools to improve—a bit more keenly than the average renter, who can more easily pick up and move to a more favorable location.

Since we are moral creatures, it's useful to think in terms of categorical imperatives: "What if everybody rented?" Would the community be better or worse for it? For the answer to that question to inform your decision on whether to rent or buy is not a bad thing. It stands to reason that when the people care about the community and the local economy, financial outcomes tend to be better.

Where should you live?

Regardless of your decision to rent or buy, you should consider a few different things when deciding on a residence. Namely, where you should live, because that single choice is going to solidify a lot of your expenses.

The cost of housing is one of the biggest sticking points with people who insist they live paycheck to paycheck. It's true that if you've locked yourself into an expensive enough mortgage or lease agreement and you're unwilling to move, you're going to keep scraping by one paycheck at a time. But if you're willing to consider downsizing, moving to a less expensive area (what we did), or moving closer to work (also something we've done), you've put yourself a couple giant leaps ahead in money management. That money being siphoned off into your gas tank or your rent payment every month is now freed up to work for you.

But geoarbitrage (that is, moving to an area with a lower cost of living) can be a double-edged sword. If you move to a low-cost of living area, chances are, you won't find high paying work. If you find high paying work, chances are, it's in a high-cost-of-living area. So, what do you do? We recommend making your decision based on your current employment.

Here are a few scenarios to help orient you as a decision-maker:

High-Income Earner Tied to a high-cost-of-living area

If you have a high-income tied to a job in a high-cost of living area, try to live *close to work*. As we detailed in Chapter 3, a long commute is not worth the mental, financial and physical sacrifices. If you need to live in a high-cost-of-living area because of your high-paying job, sacrifice the bigger home out in the 'burbs and live in a smaller apartment within walking distance of work. Although the apartment in the city may come with a premium price tag and won't be as nice as the suburban home, your savings on transportation costs and the reduced anxiety that comes with a shorter commute will likely justify this cost.

If you're renting, try to limit the damage by choosing the mediocre apartment and not the flashy unit in the new building. With your high income, your journey to FIRE can be faster if you make some small sacrifices during your wealth buildup phase. The lower your expenses are and the higher your income is, the faster your journey to FIRE will be. And once you reach FIRE, you're no longer tied to that high-cost-of-living area.

Low-Income Earner That Can Work Anywhere

If you're a low-income earner, try to move to a low cost of living area, if you're not living there already. High minimum wages can help mitigate the high cost of living, but often the drastically lower cost of living still makes a slightly lower wage worth it. Because you have a weak offense (low income), you need to focus on a strong defense (low expenses). You should also be focusing on increasing your earning potential, which doesn't necessarily equate to more schooling and more debt.

The Sweet Spot: High-Income Earner That Can Work Anywhere

The beauty of trades like plumbing and electrical work is that every city, town and country need them. You can earn a high income in Seattle and you can earn a high income in the small town of Ephrata, Washington. There are other careers that allow you to do this, like lawyers, doctors and accountants, but these careers often come with a lot of student loan debt and many years of study. Work-from-home opportunities that aren't gimmicks and can actually provide a high income in a low-cost-of-living area do pop up occasionally. But electricians and plumbers can make a high income in a low-cost-of-living area without the student loan debt a lot of us have. If you're in a career that allows you to earn a high-income anywhere, move to a low cost of living area. This will turbocharge your journey to FIRE.

Low-Income Earner Tied to a High-cost-of-living Area

This is a tough situation to be in. Maybe you're tied do a high-cost-of-living area because of family commitments or perhaps you just don't want to leave a city you love. If you're in this situation, FIRE is still possible. We were living in Seattle with wages of $13/hr.-$15/hr. and managed to save most of our take-home pay using the strategies laid out in this book. If you're in this situation, work on boosting your income, perhaps through pursuing a trade, as discussed above, or through hard work and diligence at your current place of employment. Cody transferred to his current employer from a fast food restaurant and now works as a business analyst and financial consultant from home. Though it's unfashionable nowadays to recommend you "pick yourself up by your bootstraps," a work ethic, responsibility, and diligence make up a significant portion of what it takes to increase your income.

The Impact of Nearby Family

If you're tied to a high-cost-of-living area because of family commitments, they can help to offset some of your other costs. A USDA study found that low-income families often spend less on childcare because they live close to relatives who can provide care for free.[36]

Deeply individualistic people, as Americans tend to be, might look at this setup as "mooching." We tend to think that our individual families should be self-sustaining and not rely on external support. That's a costly attitude, though. Instead of setting your family up for "independence," you're setting yourselves up for a narrower form of dependence: monetary exchange for services.

The strictly monetary view of acquiring resources might be changing as online groups like "Buy Nothing" grow in popularity, where extra resources can be donated to other members. But childcare is one of those things you don't simply hire out to a stranger—not without a thorough background check, and not without payment. The truth is that a close-knit community, and family more specifically, is the original welfare system, and the original childcare system. Community, and family in particular, play an important role in opening access to goods and services by way of loving gifts or reciprocity, which would otherwise only be available by fiscal means.

If you have trustworthy family who love you (or at least love your children), really try to see if living close to those relatives are doable, especially if you're in a high-cost-of-living area. It's not likely they'll watch your kids every weekend or even on a

[36] Mark Lino, Kevin Kuczynski, Nestor Rodriguez, TusaRebecca Schap, "Expenditures on Children by Families, 2015", *United States Department of Agriculture,* last modified March 2017, https://www.cnpp.usda.gov/sites/default/files/crc2015_March2017.pdf

weeknight, but it opens the option of occasional, inexpensive-to-free childcare. It's a twofer: Grandma or Grandpa (or Uncle and Aunt, or whomever the relative is) get to spend time with your kids, and you get to do whatever it is you need to do without the sizable babysitter fee.

We moved to the town we're in now specifically because our family lives here, and we wanted to be near family when we started ours. Having that support network has been invaluable, making it unlikely we'd ever choose to live more than half an hour away from family.

If you're fortunate enough to be a high-income earner that can work anywhere, and you have family who lives in a low-cost-of-living area, consider moving there. This combination will give you a little more momentum towards your FIRE off-ramp.

How Much Should You Spend on Housing?

As you can see, your home expense, whether renting or owning, is the most complicated expense in your budget. It depends on numerous factors. But how much should you really be spending on housing?

It depends on which of the above demographics you fall under:

1)   **High Income, High Cost of Living**: Shoot for 20% of your annual salary. If you make $100,000, this equates to $20,000 a year or $1,666/month. The better you do here, the faster you can make it to FIRE, but try to keep your rent payment or mortgage payment below this 20% figure. In this high-income/high-cost-of-living scenario, it probably makes sense to rent. Keep in mind this isn't permanent, though. This scenario allows you to put a lot of money towards your retirement nest egg. Once you hit FIRE, you can move to a lower-cost-of-living area and buy a house.

2)   **Low Income, Low Cost of Living**: Shoot for 20% here as well. If you and your spouse make $10/hour, working 40 hours a

week, your annual income will be around $41,600. This gives you about $700, which will cover a multi-bedroom apartment in a low-cost-of-living area. For instance, in Fayetteville, North Carolina, $695 will get you a 1000 square foot 2-bedroom, 2-bath unit[37].

3) **High Income, Low Cost of Living**: This is the sweet spot. Aim for 10% of your income. So, if you make $100,000/year, that's almost $1000/month. In low-cost-of-living areas, this will afford you a pretty comfortable living situation in a small house or a 2-bedroom apartment.

4) **Low Income, High Cost of Living**: 40% is what will likely be needed here to rent an apartment, but you need to hunt down the best deal you find. That might mean settling for the unit with tacky brass knobs, metal shades and appliances from the 90s. You might even consider living with roommates until you either raise your income or reduce your cost of living. If you're staying in that lower-cost-of-living area because you want to stay close to family, this factor might also help offset your high rent-to-income ratio.

The "1%" Home Ownership Rule

Keep in mind that if you choose to own instead of rent, you should include 1% of your home's value for annual maintenance/repairs in the above percentage allocations. If your house is worth $200,000, you'd want to set aside $2,000/year for maintenance expenses and reduce your mortgage budget by that amount accordingly. Some expenses can be roughly anticipated, like how many years you have left on your roof until it needs to be replaced. But other things break without warning, and you need to make room in your budget for those potential expenses. Bear in mind that for renters, landlords build these costs into the rent figure.

In any scenario, try to keep your emotions in check. A sparkling new unit or house is alluring, but consider what really makes you

---

[37] "Cross Creek Cove Apartments & Townhomes", *Apartments.com,* last modified August 10, 2018, https://www.apartments.com/cross-creek-cove-apartments-townhomes-fayetteville-nc/4nlks4k/

happy and satisfied in life after the "newness" of a housing change wears off. Do those quartz countertops create enough satisfaction to keep you working for another year? Or will the cheaper unit with laminate counters that allows you to retire a year sooner be more worth it?

Prioritize what makes you happy and build your budget from there. When you do start your housing search, don't settle for the "median" or "reasonable" price for the type of home you're looking at, as tempting as it may be. Simply avoiding getting fleeced will make you average, but finding a really good deal will put you leagues ahead in financial security and investing in your future.

Search Craigslist or a similar site for "need to sell/rent ASAP" and quickly jump on those opportunities. We found a 2-bedroom 1-bathroom unit in Ballard in 2014 for $1,050 a month with free parking and utilities. Our colleagues were paying $1,500/month for a similar unit, but we managed to score the discounted unit by replying to the ad within an hour of it being posted after seeing it was a "need to rent ASAP" opportunity. Being just a little bit smarter and quicker than the next guy will help to keep your housing and other expenses in check, which in turn helps get you to your financial goals faster.

A Final Note: House Hacking

Perhaps you live in a high-cost-of-living area where a mortgage payment would be well above the going rent for the area, but you still want to buy. Or maybe you simply want to minimize expenses as much as possible. "House hacking" is one way to reduce your housing expenses even further. Through house hacking, you'd purchase a duplex, triplex or quadplex. You'd then live in one of the units and rent out the others to offset your housing expense. Some clever hackers have paid their entire mortgage payments with their tenants' rent through this method, even managing to cover the 1% maintenance rule as well. This method can open up a sizeable income stream to supplement your savings, so it's worth some serious research if you're thinking of getting into real estate investing. If you're interested in learning more about this, we've found BiggerPockets.com and CoachCarson.com to be excellent resources.

Chapter 7

Minding the Meter

The adage "out of sight, out of mind," couldn't be truer for expenses. The convenience of paying with plastic, for instance, has a downside: it's much easier to spend more. The weight of a $200 grocery haul doesn't feel quite as heavy when you swipe your card instead of pulling out paper dollars and assorted coins. In fact, the average consumer typically spends more on a card than if they used cash.[38]

It makes sense that anything that doesn't have an immediate tangible cost might be used more often than it should, to the detriment of your bank account. Utilities are one of those things. Any individual bath or shower, or the decision to keep that A/C on constantly throughout the summer, accrues a cost. The cost for each little decision is relatively small and deferred to your next billing cycle. But as we learned in Chapter 1, little things add up to big costs, and to reach FIRE, you need to be efficient and optimized.

The average electric bill in the US in 2016 was $112.59 per month.[39] The average water/sewage/garbage collection bill in the

[38] Drazen Prelec and Duncan Simester, "Always Leave Home Without It: A Further Investigation of the Credit-Card Effect on Willingness to Pay", *New York Times*, last modified June 8, 2000, http://graphics8.nytimes.com/packages/pdf/Alwaysleavehome-2.pdf
[39] "2016 Average Monthly Bill - Residential", *U.S. Energy Information Administration,* last modified November 7, 2017, https://www.eia.gov/electricity/sales_revenue_price/pdf/table5_a.pdf

US in 2016 was $225.27 per month.[40] Together, that's nearly $350/month. That's not chump change, so we'd be wise to figure out how we can reduce these recurring expenses.

Two factors will determine how much you pay in utility bills: your location (which dictates your rate) and your usage. We have a 1,700 square foot home and pay roughly $175/month for water, sewer, trash/recycling collection, and electricity—that's nearly half of what the average consumer pays. We do this by making several smaller optimizations that add up to bigger savings with relatively little impact on our day to day comfort. Let's break down what these changes look like:

Electricity

You can slash your electricity costs almost immediately by changing a single factor: light bulbs. If you have any incandescent light bulbs in your house, buy some LED bulbs in your next grocery trip. LED bulbs used to be expensive, but now you can even find them at the dollar store. Even if you have CFL bulbs, though significantly more cost effective than incandescent bulbs, they're still no match for LED bulbs. Let's take a look at the cost difference between all three, assuming you use this light six hours a day. We'll also assume the U.S. average cost of $0.10 per kWh.[41]

Incandescent: Annual cost of $13.14
CFL: Annual cost of $3.07
LED: Annual cost of $2.19

Those are small figures, but over the long term, the difference in costs between the three is quite significant. We have to include the

"Consumer Price Index for All Urban Consumers: Water and sewer and trash collection services", *U.S. Bureau of Labor Statistics*, last modified February 14, 2018, https://fred.stlouisfed.org/series/CUSR0000SEHG
"Electric Power Monthly", *U.S. Energy Information Administration,* last modified January 24, 2018, https://www.eia.gov/electricity/monthly/epm_table_grapher.php?t=epm t_5_6_a

costs of the light bulb, though. Since LED bulbs are sold at the dollar store, the shelf prices for each type are all very comparable. But LED bulbs will often last about 20x longer than incandescent and 3x longer than CFL, meaning your $1 LED bulb will last the same amount of time as $20 worth of incandescents or $3 worth of CFLs.

The real savings are in the electricity use, though. If you multiply the annual cost difference of CFL and LED by the ten lightbulbs you might use per day, that's about $30. If you were using incandescents and swapped them out for LED bulbs, you'd be looking at about $200/year in savings after spending the $20 upfront for LED replacements.

Beyond lighting, there are several other smaller things you can implement today that can significantly cut down your electricity bill. We've organized these tips by season:

Summer

1) Set your thermostat in the mid to upper 70s, turning it off or setting it 8 degrees warmer than usual while you are away (and 8 degrees cooler in the winter). Doing this could save you up to 10% on your energy bill, according to the U.S. Department of Energy[42].

2) Don't set your thermostat to a lower temperature than you actually want. It won't cool your home any faster, but will keep the AC working longer to reach your desired temperature, wasting energy. Not only will the AC work longer, but the energy is lost faster because the temperature difference between the inside and outside of the house is greater. So only set your thermostat to the highest temperature you're comfortable with.

---

[42]"Thermostats", *energy.gov,* last modified June 2017, https://www.energy.gov/energysaver/thermostats

3) Get free air conditioning by opening your windows, shutting off the A/C, and running a fan on cooler nights. This will keep the house cooler for longer the following day.

4) When the sun comes up, close your curtains to keep as much heat out as possible.

5) If you do laundry twice a week (about 100 times a year), you'll spend about $52 on electricity a year[43]. But summer brings free heat, (aka nature's clothes dryer). If you can manage, just put your laundry through the washer and allow it to air dry in your backyard. You can buy collapsible drying racks for around $25. Store it in your laundry room and set it up on your lawn, deck or patio when you're ready to let your clothes dry. If you dry your clothes half the year, you'll about break even on the drying rack, and then start saving the following year.

    Air drying isn't for everyone though. It takes a while to hang it all up, and then you have to pull it all down again and run the dryer for ten minutes anyway to de-wrinkle your laundry. It will also fade your colored garments faster. But if you like spending time in the sunshine while not being totally useless, it can be a relaxing chore that saves a bit of money on the side.

6) Plant trees in your yard to block out the sun. Shrubs work, but as trees lose their leaves in the winter, you get the added benefit of extra sunlight when the season changes. Plus, the shade and aesthetic could add value to your property.

Winter

1) Heat escapes faster the greater the temperature differential, so the closer your internal temperature is to the external temperature, the greater the savings. Try to set your thermostat in the upper 60s so your heater doesn't run 24/7.

---

[43]"Estimating Appliance and Home Electronic Energy Use", *energy.gov*, last modified 2010, https://www.energy.gov/energysaver/save-electricity-and-fuel/appliances-and-electronics/estimating-appliance-and-home

Leave blankets on the couches, and though it should go without saying, wear socks and warm clothing. If you're used to keeping the house at 72 degrees, it will take a little while for your body to adjust, but it will, and soon 68 will be your new "normal." You'll probably find you sleep better in a cooler room, too.

2) Make sure your weather stripping is secure around your windows and doors. If you can see light around the door, it's time to replace the weather stripping.

3) Close your curtains at night to retain heat and open them back up as the sun rises.

4) Close your foundation vents (around the base of your house on the outside) and make sure you're not blocking your floor vents by keeping them closed or placing furniture over them. You don't want to pay for heat you're not getting.

You've heard it a million times before: if you're not using something, turn it off. Whether it's lights or electronics, you're shaving money off your bill with every little choice. This is a habit that requires discipline to develop so that you eventually don't have to think about it. It will become muscle memory. But you *will* forget if you don't do it consistently for a long enough period (it takes roughly two and a half months to develop a habit). Be conscientious about it and eventually switching off lights and electronics when not in use will become part of your normal routines.

Water/Sewage/Garbage

As with electricity, small changes in your day to day life could result in a major impact to these bills (except for sewage; we're not going to tell you to flush less often). Here are some things you can implement to work on reducing your usage:

1) Your lawn sprinklers probably don't need to run five days a week. Set them up to run three days a week and during rainy days, remember to turn them off so you're not watering a lawn that doesn't need it. In Mobile Alabama[44], the cost per 1000 gallons of water is $6.26. A 1200 square foot lawn watered with one inch of water (1"/week is a rule of thumb for keeping your grass green) takes 748 gallons, which costs about $4.68 a week, or a little less than $20 every month. To see how much your lawn is getting, place containers with straight sides at various points across your lawn, then measure the contents with a ruler once your sprinklers are done. If it adds up to more than an inch over the week, run your sprinklers less often, or for shorter durations. If your lawn is sprouting crabgrass or buttercups, or it puddles easily after rainfall, these are also signs your lawn is overwatered, which means there's more room for water conservation, and therefore savings.

2) For smaller zones that cover shrubs and flowers, use a watering can or hose instead of placing sprinklers to include them in their radius. By targeting the plants by hand, you'll use less water than what the more indiscriminate sprinkler will use.

3) Go with the smallest trash bin size your local garbage disposal company offers. This will result in a lower bill per month and might encourage less garbage (for instance, if you have a fireplace, your unrecyclable paper and cardboard trash can be burned). In Moses Lake, WA, a 48-gallon cart is $16.41, a 64-gallon cart is $21.87, and a 96 gallon cart is $32.81.

4) Turn your water heater down to 120 degrees. When we moved into our home, the water could scald you coming out of the tap, but we didn't address the issue until three years later. It turns out that turning down the water thermostat from 140 degrees, which is manufacturer default, can shave 6-22% off your bill

---

[44] Ben Erickson, "How to Calculate Lawn Irrigation Water Usage and Costs", *Todays Homeowner,* last modified October 10, 2007, https://www.todayshomeowner.com/calculating-lawn-irrigation-costs/

according to the US Department of Energy. You'll hardly notice a difference, practically speaking. Easy savings!

5) A little conscientiousness goes a long way. Establish conservational habits in your daily routines. For instance, if you brush your teeth while you shower, just start brushing your teeth while your water heats up instead. Small things like this and shutting the water off as you wash your face, wipe down your counters, or scrub your pots and pans, will have a big impact in the long run.

6) Don't shower every day or bathe the kids every day. To put this in perspective, say you live in Seattle where one gallon of water use is .7 cents. The average American shower is about eight minutes long and uses ten gallons of water, so that's seven cents in water costs. But heating that ten gallons of water costs[45] more than the water itself: that's 12 cents. So altogether you're out 19 cents, or nearly $70 a year. A family of four people showering every other day could save almost $140 a year, and that's not including how much you could save on soap, shampoo and conditioner.

In any case, studies show that overcleaning isn't good for you.[46] It will take a few weeks for your hair to adjust to being cleaned less frequently, but it will get less oily. Dry shampoo can help smooth the transition (particularly for the ladies), and you might find you like not having to commit to the ritual every day, or even every other day.

---

[45]"Energy Cost Calculator for Electric and Gas Water Heaters", *energy.gov,* last modified August 10, 2018 https://www.energy.gov/eere/femp/energy-cost-calculator-electric-and-gas-water-heaters-0#output
[46]Sarah Young, "Is Showering Everyday Bad for You? New Research Says Yes", *Independent,* last modified January 26, 2017, http://www.independent.co.uk/life-style/health-and-families/is-shower-everyday-good-or-bad-cleaning-hygiene-university-utah-amazon-village-microbes-skin-a7546216.html

7) Do less laundry. The older clothes washers use 40 gallons of hot water per cycle, costing 97 cents for the average American to heat the water and another 28 cents for the water. Assuming average US electricity rates, doing the "average" of eight loads of laundry a week will cost a whopping $520 a year. If you get your laundry down to twice a week (our current average as pants can be worn more than once per cleaning), it'll cost just $130 a year and save you a lot of time. But if your model is newer, it probably uses closer to 25 gallons per cycle, seven gallons of which is typically hot water (17 cents worth of electricity per load). So that's $17.68 to heat the water and $18.20 for the cost of the water for two loads a week for a year, bringing it up to a total of $35.88. Doing eight loads a week would cost you $143.52 a year.

But if you instead run your newer washer with cold water, you're just paying your water cost of 17.5 cents. It will cost you less than $18.20 a year for two loads a week, and $72 if you do eight loads a week. It's also gentler on your clothes.

If you haven't upgraded to a high efficiency washer yet, doing so will quickly regain your investment in energy and water savings.

8) Only run the dishwasher when it's full. The electricity and water together are about 18.7 cents per load. If you ran it four times a week, that's $38.90 a year. But your dishwasher isn't the only cost of getting clean dishware. We've met many people who are in the habit of "pre-washing" their dishes despite having a perfectly operational, non-archaic dishwasher. Washing dishes by hand can use eight gallons of hot water[47] on the lower end of the spectrum, or 24.6 cents. If you do a load of dishes twice a week, you're out another $25 a year by "pre-washing," plus the time it takes to do it, when you could be doing more enjoyable things. You need to use common sense,

---

[47] "Water Questions & Answers: How much water does the average person use at home per day?", *USGC,* Last Modified December 2, 2016, https://water.usgs.gov/edu/qa-home-percapita.html

of course—pans crusted with burnt cheese aren't going to get clean in the dishwasher, but don't do more work than you need to.

9) In case you're wondering, yes, paper plates cost a lot more than washing ceramic plates. You can get paper plates at Walmart for about 3.7 cents per plate. If your family uses eight plates a day, you're out about 29.6 cents. That's $108.04 a year, or almost three times what you spend on running the dishwasher (4x a week). Is it worth not having to wash (or at least rinse and put in the dishwasher) as many dishes? Some would say yes, and we don't blame them for it. For many people, their time is better spent doing things other than washing dishes: playing with the kids, going to bed a little early, finishing up some work, or doing other necessary cleaning. The question is, how much is convenience worth to you? We're not trying to guilt you into doing more dishes, but you should at least know how much more you're spending in comparison to washing plates.

Minding the meter is all about small life optimizations that can add up to a big impact. Implement some of these changes with the intent of keeping your overall utility bills around $100-$125 per 1,000 square feet. The below chart summarizes what bills you can expect, depending on the choices you make every day.

Utility Savings

Action	Washer 2x/week (hot water)	Washer 8x/week (hot water)	
Annual Cost	$35.88	$143.52	
	Washer 2x/week (cold water)	Washer 8x/week (cold water)	
Annual Cost	$18.20	$72	
	Clothes Dryer 2x/week	Clothes Dryer 8x/week	
Annual Cost	$52	$208	
	Dishwasher 4x/week	Hand-washing (10 gal. hot water)	Pre-washing (8 gal. hot water) + dishwasher 4x/week
Annual Cost	$38.90	$30.75	$63.90
	Paper plates (8/day)	Paper plates (12/day)	
Annual Cost	$108.04	$162.06	
20 bulbs/ 6 hrs. a day	LED	CFL	Incandescent
Annual Cost	$43.80	$61.40	$262.80

Chapter 8

The True Cost of Raising Kids

If you're among the many U.S. couples who are intimidated by the costs of raising a family or hesitant about whether you can have another baby, the cost of raising a child might not be as high as you think.

The very first cost accrued with children, of course, is the cost of childbirth itself. This cost can be intimidating to couples, especially since medical expenses are rather opaque and depend on many factors. It can be as much a perceived barrier to parenthood as the ongoing cost of raising a child. With employer-provided insurance, average out-of-pocket costs for vaginal delivery were $2,244 (12% of the total cost), and costs for C-section delivery were $2,669 (10% of the total cost) in 2013, according to a study by Truven Health Analytics.[48]

This data is consistent with the rule of thumb that insurance typically covers about 90% of the cost of a hospital birth. Since passage of the Affordable Care Act, all individual plans and employer-based insurance plans must offer maternity benefits.[49]

---

[48]"The Cost of Having a Baby In the United States", *Truven Health Analytics*, last modified January 2013, http://transform.childbirthconnection.org/wp-content/uploads/2013/01/Cost-of-Having-a-Baby-Executive-Summary.pdf

[49]Louise Norris, "How Obamacare changed maternity coverage", *HealthInsurance.Org*, last modified August 16, 2016, https://www.healthinsurance.org/obamacare/how-obamacare-changed-maternity-coverage/

But not all insurance plans are equally cost effective in the long run. Forecasting your expenses can help determine what plan is most cost effective for you and your family.

HSAs can be more cost effective than traditional PPO plans

A few months from our due date in 2016, we decided to crunch the numbers on whether a PPO plan or HSA plan would be more cost effective over the course of a year that includes childbirth. We knew that the HSA plan was cheaper during years we didn't have any healthcare expenses planned, but we were surprised to find out that even if delivery cost $40,000 (over double what the average hospital birth costs), it would still be more cost effective to choose the HSA plan because of the lower premiums and FICA-tax savings.

While deductibles and copays are higher for High-Deductible Health Plans (which the HSA is attached to), these plans typically have negotiated rates with providers, which means the out of pocket costs you pay will be significantly lower than "retail price." As a personal example, one of Georgi's medications, which was listed at $110, ended up being less than $10. The same held true for most of the line items on the hospital bill for our daughter's birth.

We ended up paying about $4,500 out of pocket for the delivery, which is much more than what a standard PPO plan would have us copay. But in the 16 months since, we've more than made up for the cost difference through lower premiums - about $3,200 in savings so far. Our daughter has had several checkups and immunizations since birth, but the copays have been minimal. So, while our initial cost was well above the average of $2,240 for a standard birth, in the long term we've fared better. We'll talk more about health insurance costs in Chapter 19.

There's a catch with any insurance plan, though: you need to do your research and *clarify explicitly with your insurance provider what, and who, is and is not in-network.* Even if the maternity ward is in-network, another part of the hospital that could also be providing medical attention to mother and baby might not be. For instance, the lab at our local hospital wasn't in-network. Or some of the physicians working *in* the hospital might not be covered. But you can keep unexpected costs to a minimum by having the right information. It might seem impolite to ask about costs pre and post-delivery, but unquestioningly approving every test and blood draw and spending more time in the hospital than is necessary is the easiest way to rack up the bills.

Nevertheless, delivery costs are only the beginning of nearly two decades of expenses. How much does raising a kid typically cost, and can you reasonably pay less than that to raise healthy, well-educated and well-adjusted kids?

The "Average" Cost of Child-Rearing

The U.S. Census Bureau, under contract with the Bureau of Labor Statistics, administers an annual survey called the Consumer Expenditure Survey.[50] According to the USDA, which published the survey, it's "the most comprehensive source of information on household expenditures available at the national level," surveying 23,297 married-couple households and 7,030 single-parent households, which were weighted to reflect general parenting expenditures by American families.

The final sum has been widely touted as a steep price: the estimated cost to rear a child from birth through age 17 is **$233,610** (in 2015 dollars), for a "middle-income" married couple with two kids.

Did your jaw just drop? The "middle-income" child-rearing cost of $233,610 might make one think that this is the number you should expect to pay if you want your kids to have a "middle class"

[50]Mark Lino, Kevin Kuczynski, Nestor Rodriguez, TusaRebecca Schap, "Expenditures on Children by Families, 2015", *United States Department of Agriculture,* last modified March 2017, https://www.cnpp.usda.gov/sites/default/files/crc2015_March2017.pdf

lifestyle. But that's not quite right. The range defined in the USDA report as "middle-income" is $59,200-$107,400. That's a big range for "middle-income," and it might extend beyond what you consider a "middle class" salary.

For this chapter, we'll use the figure from the report for a married couple with two children and income *under* $59,200 as a "model" middle-class family. This demographic had total costs of approximately **$164,135** per child. Is this number in the ballpark of what you should budget for, though?

Let's look at some of the real costs of raising kids, and at the end of the chapter we'll tell you how close it really is to what a reasonably frugal family is likely to spend on child-rearing.

The First Year

The first year will bring the highest cost. As shown above, the average cost of childbirth is between $2,244-$2,669. We paid about $4,500 because of our HSA plan. In addition to the upfront delivery cost, a few new recurring line items will wiggle themselves into your budget when you bring home your baby.

The first is diapers. We buy diapers for about $0.11/each. If you average about ten diapers a day during the first year, you're looking at a monthly diaper expense of $33. Add in wipes, and you're up to $40. You could save considerable coin by using cloth diapers, but like the clear majority of parents, we like the convenience of disposable diapers.

The second is your health insurance premium increase. Going from an employee+spouse plan to a family plan will likely double your premium. Chapter 19 will show you why you should choose an HSA plan over a traditional PPO plan; assuming you choose this plan, you'll likely pay between $150-$200 more per month, depending on how good your benefits are. For our purposes here, we'll go with $200/month to be on the conservative side.

Feeding Babies

Breastfeeding is primarily considered for its well-researched benefits,[51] but not buying formula will save you a lot of money: approximately $1600[52] for the first six months of your baby's life. By comparison, the cost of nursing and pumping supplies is less than $260 for the duration of your breastfeeding:

- Electric pump: $0 with insurance (current as of 2018, as mandated by the ACA)
- Handpumps (two purchased): $35
- Nursing bras: Cost was $50 for one nice bra and $80 for five acceptable ones
- Nursing pillow: $12
- Nursing pads: Average $0.40/day. If you use 2 pairs a day for the first six months, that's $72.
- Nursing cover: $10
  Total: $259

So, for the first six months of life, we saved about $1,340 by breastfeeding, and that's using estimates for the cheapest formula available in 2018.

Most women choose to supplement with formula at some point or use formula exclusively. It's a personal choice, and mothers should do whatever is best for their children given their own circumstances. If you are on the fence about whether you should stick it out with breastfeeding or unsure how much you want to supplement, you should be aware of the costs.

This is the sticker price comparison, though. In the US, a family of three earning less than $37,777 qualifies for WIC (Women, Infants and Children). WIC voucher value for formula for infants 0-3 months is approximately $65 and $80.08 for infants 4-6 months,

---

[51] "Breastfeeding Overview", *WebMD,* last modified December 5, 2017, https://www.webmd.com/parenting/baby/nursing-basics#1
[52] Kelly Bonyata, BS, IBCLC, "Financial costs of not breastfeeding...or cost benefits of breastfeeding", *Kellymom,* last modified February 8, 2018, https://kellymom.com/pregnancy/bf-prep/bfcostbenefits/#healthcare

if formula is valued at $0.8/oz. So even with WIC subsidies, formula is still going to cost over $1,450 for the first six months.

Solid Foods for Baby

So, we know breastfeeding is significantly cheaper than formula feeding, but how can you save on solid foods introduced over the first year?

Making your own baby food might sound like a lot of work, but it only requires a few hours every month to stock your freezer with several different kinds of fruit and veggie purees.

Prepackaged baby food really adds up. Jarred baby food costs about 25 cents per ounce and squeeze-pack baby food runs about 35 cents per ounce. Once your baby is almost completely off formula or breastmilk, they'll be guzzling around eight ounces a day: that's $2 worth of jarred baby food or $2.80 worth of squeeze-pack food, putting your baby food expense at about $60-84 a month.

Avoiding traditional jarred baby food, however, will keep costs under $1.20/day. Get an immersion blender and a baby food making kit (complete with reusable, freezer-safe squeeze pouches and spoon attachments) and start boiling, baking or steaming fruits and veggies. Big frozen bags of mixed veggies (around ten cents an ounce) and fruits (around 20 cents an ounce) are convenient for this. You can also mix in rice, barley or oatmeal cereal into a lot of your purees, which you can find in the baby food aisle—though we have found cereals do not fare well in the freezer. Always check the ingredients list, but you should be able to find at least one off-brand cereal with the same, or about the same, ingredients as name brands like Gerber. Buy unsweetened applesauce by the jar (5 cents/oz) and pumpkin by the can (7 cents/oz).

How Much House Do We Need for Our Family?

The next expense to consider long term is housing. The cost of raising a family varies depending on where you live. According to the report, "Families in the urban Northeast had the highest child-rearing expenses, followed by similar families in the urban West and urban South." Rural households and families in the urban Midwest spent the least on child-rearing.

As far as the physical housing goes, the USDA report found housing constituted 26-33% of a family's total expenses. The methodology assumed that each child had their own bedroom, and the cost of each bedroom occupied by a child was estimated as part of the overall cost of raising children, along with all the required furnishings like dressers and beds. This is a "conservative estimate" according to the report, since it doesn't account for the fact that, "Some families pay more for housing to live in a community with preferred schools or other amenities for children," and it doesn't account for the additional cost of a bigger yard, playrooms, or other "child-specific furnishings."

Of course, that might be a conservative estimate for how much parents *spend* on their children, but it's not a conservative estimate for how much less they *could* be spending. Sharing bedrooms is perfectly reasonable for kids, and that means you can get by with a smaller house.

Not just that, but families buying newer and bigger homes would have inflated the cost of the average bedroom in the "additional bedroom approach," since bedrooms are being built larger than in the past. Over the last couple decades, the median size of a single-family home grew by a whopping 550 square feet to 2,500 square feet. It's evident that some of this square footage increase is due to the size of bedrooms, not just the quantity. According to a 2013 survey of builders conducted by National Association of Home Builders[53], the average size of a non-master bedroom in a new

---

[53]Paul Emrath, "Spaces in New Homes", *National Association of Home Builders*, last modified October 1, 2013,

home is 481 sq. ft. For houses under 2,000 square feet total, it's still a spacious 261 sq. ft. That's 3.7x bigger than the smallest "habitable" room of 70 feet[54], and it's still more than twice the size of the previous minimum of 120 feet (a guideline established by the International Residential Code for One and Two-Family Dwellings).

Because you can choose to buy a house with smaller rooms and have children share rooms, your housing costs "per bedroom" could be much lower than the average. The median price per square foot for homes in the US is $123[55] and the average size room in a newer house under 2,000 square feet is 261 square feet. This means that extra bedroom could end up costing you $32,103. Spread over the 18 years your child will occupy that room, you'd be looking at a monthly expense of $149 per bedroom. On the other hand, you could cut the bedroom expense per child in half by having your children share rooms. Even if you eventually move to a house with more bedrooms when your children are teenagers, you could save that $149 a month (or more, depending on the number of children), for a decade (amounting to $17,880) or longer.

Clothing

Another recurring line item is clothing. Using Craigslist or buy/sell/trade groups and shopping garage sales will score you loads of clothes for around $0.50 a piece, but the downside is how time-consuming it is (unless you're buying clothes for babies or toddlers "in bulk," which you can do by hitting up just two or three garage sales, thus furnishing most of your tot's wardrobe for the next two years).

https://www.nahb.org/en/research/housing-economics/special-studies/spaces-in-new-homes-2013.aspx
[54]Michael Luckado, "Minimum Habitable Room Size Code Change", *America's Best House Plans*, last modified December 12, 2014
[55]"U.S. Home Sellers in March 2016 Realized Highest Home Price Gains Since December 2007", *RealtyTrac,* last modified April 20, 2016, https://www.realtytrac.com/news/home-prices-and-sales/march-q1-2016-home-sales-report/

A way to meet in the middle on convenience and price is consignment shopping, so see if there's a well-organized consignment clothing store near you. Goodwill is a decent option as well, though we've found their prices to be unreasonably high compared to consignment prices nearby, when you consider the fact that their supply is hopelessly unorganized, and the quality control is rather dismal. Keep in mind, though, that a substantial part of your baby's wardrobe will come from friends and family. They can't help but buy things for your kids, especially babies.

Tiny babies might need 14 outfits total, because they make a lot of messes, and seven pajama sets. But as your child grows, they need more like nine outfits total (one for every day of the week, plus two backups), and 4-5 pajamas. No matter how many clothes you accumulate, you'll find that you keep reaching for the same few outfits over and over. So, don't bother accumulating more than you think is necessary.

Kids grow fast, but by discount shopping, you shouldn't be spending more than $20/month on discounted clothes and toys.

Childcare

Of course, you'll also need breaks from the baby. Hopefully you live near family and drop off your munchkins for grandma or auntie dates, but if not, factor in another $50/month for babysitters.

One-Time Costs

One-time costs mostly have to do with prepping your nursery (changing table, dresser, crib, rocker, etc.) and some toys and books. Never buy these items new. Shop consignment or Buy-Sell-Trade groups or take items from friends and family who have outgrown their use for them. You should start looking for these things early on in your pregnancy so you have ample time to find the right items at the right price. Your initial setup shouldn't be more than $500. We got a crib and changing table for free, a dresser for $20 and a glider for $50.

Then there's the car seat and the high chair. We bought a collapsible high chair on consignment for $25 and it's held up extremely well. The car seats, however, we did buy new, though there's nothing wrong with buying or receiving a used car seat from a trusted source. The first infant car seat (for under 30 pounds or 30 inches in height) we bought for $89.99. The second, infant-to-toddler car seat was $180. Considering they do not expire for several years, we will be able to use them for the next baby, and possibly the baby after that.

So, your overall setup costs for a new baby could easily be as low as ours ($365), but $500 is a conservative estimate. Add in another $100 for checkups and you're looking at a total cost of $10,788 over the first year, including the $4,500 out of pocket delivery cost.

Year 1-3

At this point, your baby is completely on solids, but since you cook at home, you'll be able to feed them healthy, filling meals for about a dollar day. Diapers and wipes will be reduced to $35/month since you won't change as many diapers, and they should be potty-trained sometime during this stretch. Your clothes and toy budget will slightly increase to $30/month. However, your dental premiums will likely increase by about $20/month once your little one grows chompers, depending on your benefits. With insurance and childcare for date nights, your recurring monthly costs are $365/month. One-time costs won't be much. Factor in about $200 for their birthday, Christmas and transportation costs for "baby dates" and another $100 for checkups. In all, costs for years 2 and 3 are $6,468 each.

Years 3-7

No more diapers! But they're eating more now and your $35/month in savings from diapers now goes towards the food bill ($1.38/meal). Expect costs to remain around the same $6,468 per year.

Years 7-11

One-time annual costs go up to about $600 during this time as you introduce sports and other recreational activities into your kid's life. Most costs for sports done through public schools are covered by the schools, but if you homeschool, you may choose to make room in your budget for Little League or another organization not affiliated with school. Costs could range significantly, but expect to pay between $100-300 a year for basketball, soccer, baseball, martial arts, or swimming, plus gas, snacks, and gear. To be extra conservative, we'll put "extracurricular activity" costs at $600 a year, or $3,000 for five years.

Be aware that extra costs can pile on easily if your schedule is crowded with children's activities. Being away from the house all evening will mean you won't make dinner, so you might eat out. You will spend more on gas, though you might be able to share costs with other parents by carpooling. Being highly involved in competitive activities involves a considerable sacrifice of time and money for the whole family, so consider carefully before heavily investing in such extracurriculars.

On the non-competitive side of things, music lessons are a lifelong investment and the time and energy commitment for parents is much lower. Costs might be higher, depending on the teacher, the instrument, and whether they receive advanced training, but if your child reaches proficiency, he or she is much more likely to continue playing music as an adult than playing sports (though martial arts is a good lifelong investment in self-defense). An additional upside is that many resources for learning can be found for free on the internet, so you may not have to invest anything besides the initial cost of an instrument until you know your child is serious about learning to play.

Your total costs for these years should average $7,068/year.

Years 12-15

At this point, food and other non-grocery items are almost up to adult usage. In Chapter 2, we recommended spending $35/person/week. However, the more people under your roof, the lower the overall costs become as you buy in bulk. So, you should be able to feed your child healthy, delicious meals and cover non-grocery items (toilet paper, toothpaste, etc.) for $28/week. At this point, finding clothing they need, *when* they need it, for under $1/item is basically impossible. But you can keep it to an annual budget of $360 for clothes. If they want more options besides what you've bought them, they can mow lawns or babysit or walk dogs to pay for things they want.

You will also spend more on entertainment at this point (Christmas and birthday gifts, birthday parties, gifts to bring to friends' birthday parties, etc.), but this shouldn't be more than $600/year.

Add in the same annual costs of $600 for various activities like sports leagues and we're looking at $8,088/year.

Years 16-18

These years will introduce some more recurring costs, but these costs don't necessarily need to be paid for by you. Between ages 16-18, your child can get a minimum wage job and save for a car. Once they get the car, they can cover the insurance and gas payments as well as the cost of their cell phone plan. We'll assume you meet them halfway on these recurring expenses, which would equate to about $40/month. These are also the years you might go a little overboard on one-time gifts: a used car, a cell phone, a laptop, etc. High school activities also bring about higher activity costs, so your one-time costs during these years will reasonably be around the $2,000 mark (including the purchase of a used car spread out over this time frame). But at this point, you don't need to pay for childcare. So total costs come to around $9,668/year.

We won't mention college here, as we cover it in depth in Chapter 16. Just know that if you follow the strategies laid out in that chapter, you'll likely end up not needing to pay for your child's college education and they might not need to pay for it either.

So, there you have it. If we add up all these years, the cost ends up coming to $139,803, or nearly 25 grand less than the total cost estimate for "below middle income" families. This doesn't include tax benefits, though. We won't get into too much detail on some of the more unique credits, but for now consider that the Child Tax Credit will amount to $2,000/year, so you can reduce your overall costs to *$103,803*.

But wait - there'll be more!

Is that $103,803 the cost for each child in your family, though? No, it's the cost of your *first child*. When you introduce a second child into the equation, your overall costs go down. According to Pew Research Center,[56] 41% of mothers surveyed in 2014 had two children, compared to mothers who had either three (24%) or four or more children (14%). It makes sense that most of the USDA's calculations based on a two-child family would produce a "standard" cost. But interestingly, they found that the cost per child lowers the more kids you have. Each additional child costs about 24% less than the "standard" child in a two-child household.

For middle-income, married-couple households with three children, the annual expense is roughly $30,000 for all three (assuming the older children are teenagers). About $10,000 per child puts spending for middle-income households *just* above spending per child for households making below the "middle income" benchmark of $59,200. Basically, "large" middle-income families appear to spend like they aren't middle-income.

---

[56]Gretchen Livenson, "Family Size Among Mothers", *Pew Research Center*, last modified May 7, 2015, http://www.pewsocialtrends.org/2015/05/07/family-size-among-mothers/

Does that mean children from large middle-income families don't have the same material quality of life as the standard two-child families in the same income bracket? Not necessarily.

There are many reasons big families spend less and single-child families spend more. Take the initial investment in "baby gear," for instance: swings, bouncers, jumpers, car seats, etc., can be recycled for multiple children. But if you've only got one child, you can't distribute that cost among siblings.

You'll also spend less on clothes through hand-me-downs, at least while the kids are younger and they don't complain about their outfits being out of style. It turns out toddlers don't really care if their shirt is a month or a decade old, and thrifty people can find ways to save on new clothing purchases through the secondhand market.

Your health insurance premiums won't double like they did when you had your first child; in fact, they shouldn't go up at all. Baby #2 will also likely share a room with your first child, so you don't have to pay for a second bedroom. You'll spend less on food, too, since you'd buy practically everything in bulk and cook in large batches. Leftovers actually get eaten. There's less waste and less eating out (it costs a small fortune to take a big family out to a sit-down restaurant, whereas before you might not have thought twice about taking your only child out to eat). Your childcare rate also shouldn't double if you introduce another kid to the babysitter, and once your eldest is old enough, he or she can watch the younger kids in lieu of a sitter. In addition to wearing the same clothes your older child wore as a toddler, your younger child will be able to use many of the same toys.

So, if we go through all of the expenses we just laid out and removed the expenses that wouldn't apply to a second child, your second child will end up costing $60,099. After the Child Tax Credit, your total costs would be $24,099. This stays consistent with most households; the USDA survey notes that each additional child costs about 24% less than the "standard" child in a two-child household.[57]

So, having more kids is a bit like buying in bulk. It's the same quality of life for them, but you get a better deal. Having only one child, on the other hand, is like buying the smallest individual unit. Just over a fifth (22%) of mothers surveyed by Pew Research Center had only one child. On average, single-child families spent 27% *more* than two-child families, which holds steady with our personal examples.

All in all, it's entirely possible to beat the "average" cost of raising kids by tens of thousands of dollars, with your first child costing you around $6,000 a year. As of the time of this writing, our daughter (beyond the initial $4,500 delivery cost) has raised our annual expenses by about $3,360 before the Child Tax Credit, for a net increase of $1,360. We expect that once our second child comes, our costs should be even lower since our health/dental insurance premium remains unchanged with the introduction of more children and we don't plan on buying a bigger house.

Financing child-rearing is complicated and messy, just like the rest of parenthood. But there are plenty of ways your costs could be lower than the average. And who really *wants* to be average? You probably don't want to be an *average* parent; you want to be the best parent you can be. If you apply the same drive to how you handle the costs of raising kids—whether it's one child or five or whether you have one income or two, you'll probably pay much less than the "average" of $164,135 per child.

---

[57]Gretchen Livenson, "Family Size Among Mothers", *Pew Research Center*, last modified May 7, 2015, http://www.pewsocialtrends.org/2015/05/07/family-size-among-mothers/

Chapter 9

Self-Care

So far, we've talked about how to lower costs for groceries, entertainment, transportation, housing, utilities, and even raising kids.

But we have yet to cover a comparably small but nevertheless important expense: self-care. Here, we mean self-care as encompassing anything you do to maintain good hygiene and to make yourself look or feel better, from soap, to haircuts, to workout gear and gym memberships.

Compared to housing, whatever you're spending right now on self-care is probably peanuts. But like eating out, this expense can easily balloon out of control, mostly because they tend to form habits instead of being the occasional splurge. We live in a very self-focused culture, particularly since the inception of Instagram and selfie-sticks. We're constantly encouraged to "treat yo self."

Every ad department of every beauty and personal care franchise out there is telling you "you're worth it." You probably believe "you're worth it." And maybe that's true, but the question that must be addressed is: what are their products and services worth *to you?*

Because the color treatments and the manicures or the pricey beard oil aren't always going to be worth it. Especially if you're trying to get out of debt.

So, let's talk about some ways you can recharge and stay fresh for less. All those dollars and cents are going to add up in the long run, especially if you're starting from a typical middle-class lifestyle, and yes, *especially* if you're a woman.

Modern Womanhood is Pricey

Money Magazine estimated that women spend an average of $15,000 on makeup over her lifetime, and roughly $43 per makeup shopping trip.[58] If you live to be 80, that's $15 a month. But that's chump change compared to what women spend on their dos. A survey from lookfantastic.com found that the average woman spends $80 a month on hair care.[59]

According to calculations done by Statista in 2017 based on the Simmons National Consumer Survey (NHCS) and U.S. Census data, the majority of Americans (74.69 million) spent less than $50 on skincare in the last three months, but nearly 41 million Americans spent $50-99.[60] If you're spending $25 a month on skincare, you're under 35, and your skin is relatively unproblematic, you're probably spending more than you need to.

But even if you leave skin care costs aside, the sum of the average made up face and hairdo is $95 a month. That's more than your phone bill and probably more than your cable bill (that is, if you still have a cable bill).

---

[58]Colleen Kraftofil, "Can You Guess How Much a Woman Spends on Makeup in Her Lifetime? (We Were Way Off!)", last modified March 30, 2017, http://people.com/style/how-much-does-a-woman-spend-on-makeup/

[59]Sarah Ferguson, "How expensive is your hair? A new survey finds that the average woman in the U.S. will spend over $55,000 on grooming and styling in her lifetime", *DailyMail,* last modified June 23, 2017, http://www.dailymail.co.uk/femail/article-4633248/How-Money-Women-America-Spend-Hair.html

[60]"U.S. population: How much money did you spend on skin care products in the last 3 months?", *Statista*, last modified 2017, https://www.statista.com/statistics/317876/us-households-total-amount-spent-on-skin-care-products-past-3-months/

Without getting into nitty gritty price comparisons, here are some simple things you can do to reduce your self-care costs:

1. Don't dye or treat your hair

It's virtually impossible to spend $80 a month with cuts from Great Clips and basic drugstore care products. $80 a month is for people who dye or perm their hair. We understand that some people's curly hair is hard to tame if it isn't semi-permanently straightened or perhaps braided, but for the rest of you, consider going back to your natural hair. Not only will you save the $75 your spending on regular color treatments (every eight weeks, if you're really stretching it), but you'll save on all the other products you use to counter the negative effect they have on your hair.

2. Get low-end haircuts

It's nice to be pampered occasionally, and boutique salons offer a pleasant, relaxing experience along with the more highly skilled hair stylists. If you're dying your hair, you're probably going to a boutique full-service salon anyway.

You should stop. Or at least, you should limit your "nice" haircuts to once or twice a year. Georgi has done this for years. She gets a cut & style at a mid-range salon about once a year and goes to franchise hair salons for cheap trims in between.

$45, the average price of a woman's haircut according to data from Square[61] (on the very low end for boutique salon cuts), is a lot to pay 4-6 times a year. Even if you're only getting a trim at a boutique salon, it's still going to cost you more than a full cut from the franchise salon.

---

[61] Tom Risen, "What America Pays for a Haircut", *U.S. News & World Report*, last modified February 28, 2014, https://www.usnews.com/news/blogs/data-mine/2014/02/28/what-america-pays-for-a-haircut

3. Do your mani-pedis at home

For a $15 manicure, you could buy one or two salon quality nail lacquers to use at home that will last you at least 40 manicures. Manis are a fun thing to do with friends and family, and maybe you'll still have a couple mani-dates a year. But to maintain manicured nails all the time is a $30/month commitment easily. Acrylic nails are a twice-a-month affair that's going to cost at least $40/session.

Barring some basic nail tools and a few bottles of good polish, manicures are a completely unnecessary expense. If we're being honest, salon manicures belong in the "entertainment" category of the budget, not in self-care.

4. Limit purchases of high-end makeup

A preference for high-end makeup (the kind you find in Sephora, Macy's or Nordstrom) is going to easily cost you double or quadruple the price of comparable products at the drugstore or your local Walmart. If there's a product you find particularly hard to part with, the internet will yield tons of videos comparing drugstore "dupes" to your high-end favorites. Of course, some of us have skin problems that drug store products won't meet, and in that case, you shouldn't feel guilty about buying high end products that do address your particular problems. But at least do some research, be patient in waiting for sales, and try to score some coupons if you can.

5. Don't "browse" cosmetics

Especially at high end retailers. The more time you spend shopping, the more products you're going to want. As an example, Georgi didn't even know what "highlighter" was in the cosmetic world until someone told her about it in her early 20s. For years, she only stepped into the beauty aisles to restock on items she had run out of in her minimal kit or pick up an $8 eyeshadow palette. But the more time you spend looking at products, the more your current repertoire will feel inadequate. That's why it's best, if you have a shopping habit, to limit your shopping trips and limit browsing while in the store. When you say, "I'm just going to browse," what you almost always mean is, "I want to buy something—I just don't know what yet." And that's a really good way to waste your money on things you don't need.

Men can save, too!

Men typically don't spend nearly as much on self-care as women, but it doesn't mean there isn't room for savings. If you're buying razors with seven blades and two moisturizing strips and replacing the blades frequently, shaving costs can really add up.

For example, if you were subscribed to Gillette Fusion ProShield in 2017, four cartridges would put you out $21.45. That's nearly the price of one of our cell phone bills. By contrast, for us to receive four multi-blade, high-quality razors each month from Dollar Shave Club, we pay $6, tax included. And we're quite satisfied with the results.

But obviously you need to use shaving cream or shave oil or a high-lather soap, and those can range in price, too. If you're spending $5 for a shave lubricant when you could be spending $1, that $4 a month can add up over time. And while aerosol shave creams are convenient, the better value is often in shave soaps you lather with a brush. Like we talked about in the first chapter, you should do some research and do these sorts of calculations with pretty much anything you buy on a recurring basis. As we established in chapter 1, reducing or eliminating recurring expenses have the double effect of decreasing your expenses now and reducing the amount you need to save for retirement.

But we can't forget about the bearded among us. Beard trims cost about $15. If you're accustomed to being at the barbers' for trims every month (or even every fortnight), that's going to cost you at least $180 a year. Consider trimming at home. As for beard oils and balms, they tend to range from $2 to $20 for an ounce, which will last about three months. There might be room to shave off a few dollars there.

The biggest regular self-care cost for men is the haircut. A $18 cut at a franchise salon may not seem like a big purchase, but as we keep saying, the costs add up. A few years into our marriage, we decided we'd had enough of forking over our cash for a very simple haircut. Cody had enough faith in his wife to hand her a $30 shave kit and some scissors to do the job herself, and we haven't looked back since. In the past three years, we've saved at least $400 (since he was getting a trim every six weeks). At least.

So, if your significant other has a steady hand, consider doing haircuts at home. It's a time saver, too, because even if it takes twice as long to cut their hair, you don't have to travel to and from the barber.

What About Exercise?

The average American with a gym membership (one in five Americans) spends $54 a month on it[62], roughly 1.2% of the average income. Of course, there are budget gyms that will cost around $20 a month, but that's still $240 a year.

If you instead invested the $20 a month you were spending on the "budget" gym membership, you'd have over $3,500 after ten years. If you had the average gym membership and instead invested that $54/month, in ten years you'd have nearly $9,500.

Of course, we need to take care of our bodies, and exercise is critical to that. But a gym membership *isn't worth it*. You might say, "Well, it's convenient to have all the exercise equipment I could ever need in one place," but your goal is not access to expensive resistance-training machines, it's to be in shape. And you don't need all that gear and equipment to do that.

---

[62] Samuel Becker, "Gym Membership Costs: The Facts Your Gym Won't Tell You", *Health and Fitness Cheat Sheet,* last modified July 3, 2017, https://www.cheatsheet.com/health-fitness/gym-membership-costs.html

Cody lost over 45 pounds without a gym membership. He set up a small training area in the garage with a mat, weights, an exercise bike, and a pull-up bar. We invested in quality running shoes for him (they were discontinued so Georgi found him a killer deal on Amazon) and he went on a run every other day for months. As for Georgi, she used the stationary bike that was given to us along with an ab machine, a $10 yoga mat, and a YouTube channel for at-home workouts.

Running, especially if you live in a hilly area, is the cheapest way to boost your metabolism and shed the weight. The downside is....it's running. Running in the rain and the biting cold is no fun (and inhaling very cold air can be bad for your lungs). Honestly, poor weather is more of a barrier to exercise then getting in the car to drive to the gym. So, if your winters are cold and miserable, find a cheap treadmill in a Buy Sell Trade group or a garage sale. People are always selling off their old exercise equipment because they don't have room for it anymore, or they've bought newer equipment to replace it.

If you feel like you need to be weight-training, garage sale season will yield dozens of dirt-cheap options for this as well. The dumbbells you pick up for $7 a piece are not going to lose any more value between this spring and the next, so you don't have a lot to lose. Even the treadmill you find has likely hit the bottom of its depreciation curve (just like with cars, do your research and don't get suckered), and if you don't feel you've gotten enough use out of it, you can sell it without too much loss.

But honestly, you probably don't need any gear at all. You need $10 stretchy-pants, a sports bra (if you're a woman), a yoga mat and YouTube. Thousands of free workout routines from traditional push-ups and crunches, to Pilates, to hip-hop are available *for free*.

You might argue the gym membership keeps you accountable because you don't want to waste your monthly due. But if you can burn the same number of calories and build the same amount of muscle at home virtually for free, how is it worth your money, even if you do use the gym multiple times a week?

Not to mention, you're likely spending way more than your gym membership on your fitness. Gyms are centers for consumerism, selling you branded gear, expensive smoothies, and supplements. The more time you spend there, the more pressure you will feel to conform. You start to feel like you need new shoes, new leggings, new bras, tank tops and branded stainless steel water bottles so you don't feel like a ragamuffin in hand-me-downs who doesn't belong with the shiny people. Ultimately, it's a place of heightened self-consciousness, with mirrors everywhere and at least a half dozen other bodies to compare yourself against. Maybe that drives some people to work even harder, but we find it hard to believe it works that way for most people, especially if their goal weight or measurements are a long way off.

So, don't buy gym memberships. Invest in home exercise instead and put the rest into your retirement accounts.

Just for illustrative purposes, let's add up the monthly costs of some typical self-care expenditures of a man and a woman:

Man	
Current	**Recommended**
1 can shave cream: $5	Shave cream/soap: $1
Razors: $20	Razors: $3
Haircut: $15	Haircut: $0
Skincare: $16	Skincare: $5.33
Exercise: $35	Exercise: $8*
Woman	
Current	**Recommended** Woman: Color treatment: $0

Color treatment: $45 (average cost if it's an every-other-month affair) Manicure: $25 (two appointments/mo.) Makeup: $15 Razors: $20 Skincare: $16 Haircut (average 6/yr.): $25 Exercise: $35	Manicure: $0 Makeup: $5 Razors: $3 Skincare: $8 Haircut (average 4/yr.): $10 Exercise: $8* *a monthly average of initial investments in inexpensive gear. Eventually they "pay for themselves."
Current total for man and woman: **$247**	Recommended total: **$46.33**

That's a difference of $200.67. How much would this amount to if it compounded daily for ten years at 7% interest? $35,155.[63] In addition, following the 4% rule, you'd need to save an additional $60,200 to cover this expense post FIRE. In all, you're looking at an impact of nearly **$95,200**. Assuming you make the median salary of $44,564,[64] are these extra products and services worth working an extra two years for?

It's hard to say exactly what you should be spending without knowing your specific situation, but for low-maintenance people (people without moderate or severe acne, psoriasis, or other skin problems, and people with low-maintenance hair types) less than $18/month for men and around $33/month for women should adequately cover your basic needs.

---

[63] "Compound Interest Calculator" *U.S. Securities and Exchange Commission,* last modified August 25, 2016, https://www.investor.gov/additional-resources/free-financial-planning-tools/compound-interest-calculator

[64] "Table 3. Median usual weekly earnings of full-time wage and salary workers by age, race, Hispanic or Latino ethnicity, and sex, fourth quarter 2017 averages, not seasonally adjusted", *Bureau of Labor Statistics,* last modified January 17 2018, https://www.bls.gov/news.release/wkyeng.t03.htm

Chapter 10

Creating Your Surplus

The last 9 chapters have covered most controllable recurring expenses. It's very possible, in fact likely, that there is an expense you have that we didn't address. Maybe this expense is necessary and cannot be reduced or eliminated, or perhaps it's a one-off expense. Here are some expenses you may be thinking of:

1) **Health/Dental/Vision**: Although we covered these premiums in Chapter 8 for your children, we didn't discuss the cost of health insurance to you. We didn't cover this in depth because it's not really an expense you can control during the wealth-building stage, assuming your insurance comes from your employer. Whatever rates your HR team sets, you'll likely just need to pay those rates. There *is* some wiggle room here with HSA plans and we'll cover exactly what that looks like in Chapter 19 and why HSA plans will almost always be a better option than traditional PPO plans. [65] With this in mind, let's look at what you should expect to pay with one of these plans.

   According to the Employer Health Benefits Survey, the average cost for an employee's premium on an HSA plan is about $85/month. Data wasn't available for premium costs for employee+spouse plans, but we'll assume they'll double to $170/month. Preventative care is covered completely under

---

[65]"2017sw Employer Health Benefits Survey", *The Henry J. Kaiser Family Foundation*, last modified September 19, 2017, https://www.mercer.com/newsroom/national-survey-of-employer-sponsored-health-plans-2016.html

HSA plans, meaning you won't pay anything for your annual checkup. Assuming the occasional broken bone, unexpected ER visit and prescription, we'll budget $25/month/person for health costs, on top of your premium. If this seems low, keep in mind that your employer will likely contribute to your HSA plan on top of whatever they contribute for their share of premium costs! In our experience, this is between $30-$60/month. So, although premiums are completely dependent on your health insurance, we'll assume $110/month/person in health costs during your working career. Dental will add about $30/month/person and vision shouldn't be more than $10/month/person. In all, $150 a month per person should be reasonable for most.

2) Another potential expense is **tithing**. If you're a church or synagogue member, chances are your sending 10% of your paycheck to your congregation. As with health insurance, we differ from the norm when it comes to tithing. As opposed to giving 10% of our paycheck, we give 10% of our expenses during the wealth-building phase. Once we hit FIRE and live off of our investments, we plan to continue to give 10% of our expenses, allowing us to tithe indefinitely. Since a lot of Americans that tithe 10% of their paycheck promptly spend their full paycheck, the effect is roughly the same. This is our conviction when it comes to tithing, but you'll have to work out what you believe is appropriate.

3) Gifts are another expense that crops up year over year for various birthdays, parties and Christmas. Instead of having everyone buy a gift for every member of the family, consider doing a family gift exchange during the holidays, and keep birthday presents limited to immediate family members. This shouldn't end up costing more than $100/month/household. Since we already included the cost of presents for your kids in Chapter 8, we don't need to create a separate line item here.

4) We covered some electronics and other entertainment expenses in Chapter 4, but we haven't covered costs like

furniture, clothing and other electronics that most of us buy for ourselves (though we did discuss what these should look like for your kids). We tend to buy these items for the long term. Although a pair of $75 shoes is triple the cost of what you can find at the local discount shoe store, those $75 shoes will likely last ten times longer. We have a household policy that anything that separates you from the ground (shoes, mattresses, chairs and couches) should be high quality.

Take mattresses for example. There is no other product you can buy that will take up more of your time. You spend a third of your life, maybe more, on your mattress. If your mattress lasts you ten years (nearly 30,000 hours,) you should opt for the new $750 mattress that won't kill your back over the $250 Craigslist used mattress, even though the savings might be screaming to you that the cheaper option is obviously superior. But really, that $500 difference represents less than $0.02/hour of use. If you wake up with back pain because of your mattress, ask yourself this: would you have paid 14 cents for an amazing night's sleep last night? If the answer is yes, buy a quality mattress.

You should also buy quality chairs, couches and shoes. Chances are you'll even save money in the long run, as you don't need to replace high-quality items nearly as often. And keep in mind that high-quality items don't have to be brand new. Although we recommend buying your mattress new, you can find high-quality sofas on Craigslist for $200-$300 that could last decades.

As for clothing, shirts can be found at thrift stores or during Black Friday sales for a few dollars each. Pants will probably be around $30. Coats and jackets can be snagged at the thrift store for $10-$20. Keep in mind that shopping off-season in general will save you money: buy summer clothes on clearance in winter, and winter clothes on clearance in summer.

Moving on, technology and toys probably keep you pacified, but they don't actually bring that much joy. Sure, having a TV and a gaming console is nice, but having a PS4, Xbox One *and* Nintendo

Switch is completely unnecessary. We've already covered how you can get phones on the cheap; beyond that, a high-quality laptop might hit you for $500-$1,000, but should last a long time.

For clothing, furniture, electronics, budget roughly $60/month/person. If you're married, this is nearly $15,000 every ten years and should be more than enough to cover these three expenses.

A note on pets

Pets are important, too, and far be it from us to tell you to banish a member of your family. The costs of most common pets are relatively small, unless you are taking Fluffy to the groomers or putting her in doggy daycare on a regular basis—in that case, try to find cheaper alternatives. For the low-maintenance animals, a $20-$30 bag of pet food and a few bucks for grooming supplies every six months can be added to your grocery budget.

Our chihuahua-maltese dog Pilot has long, wiry hair and a penchant for mischief. (Adorably, he once tore a bell pepper off our plant and played with it in the backyard for hours.) Georgi trims the hair around his face every few months with regular scissors and together we clip his claws. Our toddler, Eloise, likes to "brush" him regularly. When we're out of town, he either comes with us or stays at either set of our parents' house—both enjoy having him. Other than that, he's pretty low maintenance. In general, pets are valuable for the work we put into them, both emotionally and in terms of teaching your kids responsibility.

At this point, we should have touched on most reasonable expenses people have. Maybe we didn't cover your $20/month gaming crate or your $50/year collection of magazine subscriptions. If you have any of these or any other "just for fun" expenses that don't provide any real value to you, you should cut those expenses immediately.

Here's a summary of what your major expense categories could look like after implementing the tips and strategies thus far:

Single

Groceries/Non-Food Items: $150/month
Phones/Cable/Internet: $100/month
Entertainment/dates: $40/month
Transportation Costs: $150/month
Utility Costs (assuming 750 square feet): $85/month
Self-Care: $25/month
Health/Dental/Vision Costs, including insurance: $150/month
Clothes/Furniture/Electronics: $100/month
Presents: $100/month

Married Couple

Groceries/Non-Food Items: $300/month
Phones/Cable/Internet: $125/month
Entertainment/date nights: $75/month
Transportation Costs: $150/month
Utility Costs (assuming 1,500 square feet): $170/month
Self-Care: $30/month
Health/Dental/Vision Costs, including insurance: $300/month
Clothes/Furniture/Electronics: $120/month
Presents: $100/month

Total Costs Before Housing/Children/Tithing for a Single Person: $900/month
Total Costs Before Housing/Children/Tithing for a Married Couple: $1,470/month

Housing costs are dependent on which of the four demographics laid out in Chapter 6 you fall under. As a ballpark estimate, we'll assume $1,050/month for our married couple. This gets you a 2-bed/1-bath apartment in Seattle (if you find a really good deal) or a 2-bed/1-bath house in Spokane, WA. For our single person, we'll assume $700/month. This gets you a studio apartment in Seattle or a 2-bed/1-bath apartment in Spokane.

Total Costs Before Children/Tithing for a Single Person: $1,600/month

Total Costs Before Children/Tithing for a Married Couple: $2,520/month

So, there you have it: annual expenses totaling $30,240 for a married couple or $19,200 for a single person. If you have kids, add $500/month for your first child, $100/month for your second, $250/month for your third (increased cost due to needing an additional bedroom) and $100/month for your fourth. Through this, this is what your annual expenses could reasonably look like for most demographics:

Single: $19,200
Couple: $30,240
Couple with 1 Child: $36,240
Couple with 2 Children: $37,440
Couple with 3 Children: $40,440
Couple with 4 Children: $41,640

And if you tithe:

Single: $21,120
Couple: $33,264
Couple with 1 Child: $39,864
Couple with 2 Children: $41,184
Couple with 3 Children: $44,484
Couple with 4 Children: $45,804

These expenses do represent the higher end of the scale. We know that if you're committed, you can live around $30,000/year very comfortably with multiple children, even if you tithe. We know this because we live below $30,000 a year very comfortably in a 3-bed/2-bath, fully renovated home with a child and a dog, and we love our life.

If you cannot get your expenses below $30,000 for you and your spouse, that's okay, too. This $30k threshold allows you to hack college funding (we'll discuss this later), but it doesn't mean you can't hit FIRE if you spend more. You'll still retire decades before your peers, but it'll take a little longer. As we'll cover in a later chapter, your timeline to retirement depends on two factors: your savings rate and your post-FIRE expenses.

Once you've reduced your expenses, you'll be spending significantly less than what you make. This surplus is what's going to get you to FIRE. It may be pocket change now, but once you pay off your consumer debt, that surplus will drive your investments month over month. The quicker you can get to the investment stage, of course, the shorter your journey to early retirement will be. So, the next chapter will be all about how to buckle down and pay off your debt, which is a sweet financial freedom in itself.

Chapter 11

Debt Payoff

Now that you've created a surplus of funds by cutting your expenses, you need to pay off your consumer debt. According to data compiled by Nerdwallet[66] from the Federal Reserve Bank of New York and the U.S. Census Bureau, the average U.S. household owes $15,654 in credit card debt, $173,995 in mortgage debt, $27,669 in auto loan debt and $46,597 in student loan debt.

This means the average household has roughly $90,000 in consumer debt (credit cards, auto loans and student loans). This number isn't surprising—we had roughly the same amount of debt (excluding the mortgage), even with each of us graduating high school with two years of college under our belts. At our highest point, we were paying about $1,250 in monthly minimum payments. Fortunately, we didn't have any credit card debt, but our interest rates on our private student loans and our car loan were pretty high.

This $1,250 had to be paid for using after-tax dollars, meaning we needed to earn about $1,500/month just to make the monthly payments—even living in Washington, which doesn't have a state income tax. Most Americans know only too well how hard it can be to make ends meet when the budget has been stretched thin over so many minimum payments. This is why debt is so detrimental to building wealth.

---

[66] Erin El Issa, "2017 American Household Credit card Debt Study," *Nerdwallet,* last modified December 11, 2017, https://www.nerdwallet.com/blog/average-credit-card-debt-household/

So, before we start getting into investments that will grow your wealth, we need to address the heavy, hideous monster you've had strapped to the roof of your budget: debt.

You have a plethora of books, sites and resources about debt payoff to choose from, each recommending slightly different strategies and ranging from chipping away twenty bucks at a time to attacking it with every single spare penny you can manage. But ultimately, it comes down to individual effort and how badly you want it. Consolidation and methodology are meaningless if you don't put in the effort and hard work needed to get your net worth out of the negatives.

Getting to that point is really when the wealth building journey begins. As we discussed in the opening chapters, the first thing you must do is stop buying crap you don't need. But overcoming the cultural gravity that pulls everyone and their dog toward consumerism at the expense of financial health isn't easy. We're constantly bombarded with new products and fancy services that can be paid for later. With ads boasting "five easy payments" and "pay no interest for ten years," the process of "buying" (what you're really doing is financing) things gets easier and easier. The dopamine rushes we get from satisfying our instant gratification urges is seductive, but you *will* eventually get to the point where the monthly bills are uglier than the new purchases are alluring. You will need to pay those things off eventually. Instead of putting your head in the sand and saying Future You will take care of it, you need to be Future You *now* and develop some self-discipline.

Paying off debt isn't easy and the feeling you get isn't nearly as intoxicating as driving off the lot with a newly-financed car. We don't have any magic formula or strategy that will make this process any more fun, but we can tell you what worked for us and our 20-month payoff of over $83,000 of consumer debt.

Debt Snowball vs. Debt Avalanche

These are the two most common debt payoff strategies. One makes more sense mathematically and one makes more sense psychologically. The "debt snowball" as characterized by popular finance guru Dave Ramsey proposes applying whatever surplus you have towards the debt with the smallest balance. Once that's paid off, you take that same surplus, plus the little added on top from the no-longer-needed monthly payment on the recently eliminated debt, and apply that package to your next lowest balance debt. You continue this until your debt is wiped out. The more loans you payoff, the greater your surplus becomes, and the faster you pay off debt - that's why it's called a snowball. Here's a dummy debt load for illustrative purposes:

Dummy Debt Load

	Balance	Monthly minimum
Debt #1	$500	$25
Debt #2	$1,500	$25
Debt #3	$3,000	$200
Debt #4	$25,000	$450
Debt #5	$35,000	$550

Now, let's assume the debt holder has a $1,000 monthly surplus to put towards debt, in addition to the monthly minimums:

Sample Debt Snowball Payoff

Mo.	Action	Surplus
1	Pay off debt 1, put $500 towards debt 2	$1,025/month
2	Pay off debt 2, put $25 towards debt 3	$1,050/month
5	Pay off debt 3, put $175 towards debt 4	$1,250/month
25	Pay off debt 4, put $175 towards debt 5	$1,700/month
45	Pay off debt 5	$2,250/month

There you have it. A simple $1,000 monthly surplus can pay off $65,000 worth of debt in less than four years, even if 100% of your monthly minimum payments goes towards interest. In reality, the debt payoff timeline will take even less time, as it's likely some of your monthly minimum payment will go towards the principal balance.

The debt avalanche method, however, is mathematically superior. It states that you should pay off your highest-interest debt first. While this will make your overall debt payoff journey faster, if your highest-interest debt is debt 5 in the example above, it will take you nearly three years to pay off your first debt, and that could be discouraging. After paying off that large loan, however, your debt balance plummets rapidly, which is why it's referred to as an "avalanche." It takes some time to get going, but once it starts to move, it goes quickly.

We utilized the debt snowball method for the psychological benefit. Through this method, we were able to see our surplus grow faster and our individual debts paid off sooner, even though it did take us an extra couple months to pay off our overall debt than if we had employed the debt avalanche strategy.

Regardless of which method you choose, you have to eliminate consumer debt before you can start building wealth. It is an emergency and needs to be treated as such.

But should you always pay off consumer loans? If you have a loan that has an interest rate of 3%, and after finding out later in this book (spoiler!) that the market returns, on average, 7% after inflation, shouldn't you keep that debt and use that money to gain higher returns in the market?

Well, it depends. We tend to advocate that your living expenses should be as low as possible, preferably below the $30,000/year range for your household ($20,000 if you're single), plus $6,000/year for your first child and roughly $1,800/year on average for each additional child to maximize certain strategies laid out in future chapters. If you have $15,000 in annual debt payments all going towards loans that are below a 3% interest rate and another $15,000 in annual mortgage payments, living under $30,000 is impossible. So, while you technically can and will likely get greater returns in the market over paying off low-interest debt, we'd still recommend paying off all consumer loans. But if you decide you want to keep your 3% student loan and get your investment career started early, it's not a stupid move.

If, on the other hand, you decide to keep your 22% interest loan and start investing, that *would* be a stupid move. Anything under 7% can be debated; anything over it, pay that debt off and collect your guaranteed return.

Another note about double-digit-interest debt: if you have any, we strongly recommend you live on a tight budget until you at least rid yourself of that high interest debt. Each day you tow that enormous debt monster is another day of spinning your wheels, trying vainly to gain some traction. While we're not advocating living on a shoestring budget indefinitely, we do recommend doing so when you have high-interest debt.

Loan consolidation: is it worth it?

If we're talking about consumer debt that will take more than five years to pay off, loan consolidation is worth considering. Generally speaking, though, we advocate for aggressive debt payoff, which will make the money saved on consolidated interest relatively minute, as your payoff period shouldn't last more than a few years. Consolidating debt also takes the debt snowball and debt avalanche methods out of play, removing a great psychological boost during a challenging time.

Should I have an emergency fund?

Emergency funds are advocated by advisors like Dave Ramsey, and for good reason: it's there to make sure an emergency doesn't throw your finances into chaos. But as risk averse as we are, we hate inefficiency. While we understand the security granted by having a cash cushion of 3-6 months' worth of expenses, that money set aside in a normal bank account for emergencies is just sitting there, earning an interest rate that probably doesn't even cover inflation.

Let's say your monthly expenses are $3,000 and you want six months' worth of expenses saved up, for a total of $18,000. Let's also assume you're 20 and decide to keep this $18k cushion (which would slowly decrease in value due to inflation) over your ten-year path to FIRE. If instead you invested that over your ten year journey, it would've grown to over $36,000, leaving you with an opportunity cost of $18,000.[67] That extra security may have cost you another five months working a job you might hate, based on the average American salary.[68] It's comforting to have in case you

[67]"Compound Interest Calculator" *U.S. Securities and Exchange Commission,* last modified August 25, 2016, https://www.investor.gov/additional-resources/free-financial-planning-tools/compound-interest-calculator

[68]"Table 3. Median usual weekly earnings of full-time wage and salary workers by age, race, Hispanic or Latino ethnicity, and sex, fourth quarter 2017 averages, not seasonally adjusted", *Bureau of Labor Statistics,* last modified January 17 2018, https://www.bls.gov/news.release/wkyeng.t03.htm

have a sudden job loss, but after investing for a year, you should have enough money in equities to cover absolute emergencies. So, you *do* have a cushion, just not in your regular bank account.

Security is a powerful thing, though, so here's a middle option: Once you've saved your first $18,000 or whatever you feel comfortable having in your emergency fund, put it in your savings account and don't invest it. Once that's done, start investing in your taxable brokerage account with each additional dollar of surplus you generate. When the balance of your taxable brokerage accounts matches what you have in your emergency fund, transfer your full emergency fund into your taxable brokerage account. This way, even if the market plunges 50%, you'll still have your original emergency fund, plus it will go even farther with the deflation that tends to come about with a market crash (we'll cover deflation in a future chapter). Through this method, your $18,000 doesn't sit idle for too long, yet you can still rest assured that you can pull your emergency fund from your taxable account if needed.

When you're just starting out, your debt can be intimidating. But don't neglect it and pass it off for Future You to handle when things get bad. You need to cut this trailer full of misery from your tow as soon as possible so you can head toward your off-ramp at maximum velocity.

Chapter 12

Travel Hacking

Now that we've got the debt portion squared away, let's talk about one more cost-cutting technique. We didn't want to include this tool in the earlier expense-reduction chapters as it involves three prerequisites:

1) Your consumer debt must be paid in full
2) You must have a good credit score (above 700)
3) You must be able to pay your credit card balance on time and in full in each month

If *any* of these three don't apply to you, skip this chapter. Don't sign up for credit cards if you struggle with paying off a credit card in full and on time every month.

That said, let's get into travel hacking. When we were first starting our journey to FI, we knew we wanted to do some traveling post-retirement and we were having difficulty building this expense into our final FIRE number. That is, the amount we would need to have saved up to consider ourselves Financially Independent. We figured some years would have little to no travel expenses, some years might accrue $1-$2,000 in expenses and if we ever wanted to take an international trip, the expense would be much higher. Feeling stuck, we started digging for ways to reduce and plan for travel expenses post retirement. That's when we stumbled onto the concept of travel rewards.

Like most people, we already knew a little about frequent flyer miles, but we took it at face value (that is to say, literally): we thought you had to "fly frequently" to get anything worthwhile. Knowing we're only on a plane once a year at most, we wouldn't fly enough to get "frequent flyer miles" for any sort of free or discounted flights.

Take Alaska Airlines miles, for example. You get one flight mile for each mile you actually fly, and 25,000 miles gives you a standard domestic roundtrip flight for free. Let's say you fly from Seattle to Denver, round trip. That's 2,048 miles that go towards your "balance." You'd have to take that round-trip flight 13 times to have earned enough miles to book the same flight for free! Most travel reward credit cards also give you one mile per dollar spent. Under this principle, you'd need to spend $25,000 to get that free domestic round-trip flight or a combination of spending and flying.

For the average person who doesn't put $25,000 on a credit card quickly or doesn't fly very often, banking on travel rewards to reduce expenses might seem silly. And if these were the only two options of earning travel rewards, we'd agree. But as we've discovered, there's a much faster way to earn miles: **card opening bonuses.**

We're sure you've seen the flyers in the mail that state, "Sign up for our card and get 30,000 miles!" and promptly discarded them as junk. If you meet the three prereqs above, though, you may want to think twice about throwing these offers away. You don't even need to wait for the ads to arrive in the mail; a plethora of sites provide signup links for the highest-bonus offer on each card.

But just how valuable can these points be? Let's look at the CSP (Chase Sapphire Preferred) card. As of this writing, if you sign up for this card *and spend $4,000 in the first three months*, you will get their sign-up bonus of 50,000 Chase Ultimate Reward points. For each and every card that offers bonus points upon card opening, you must meet some sort of minimum spend. Most of the time, it's about $3,000 within the first three months of card opening, but it can be as low as a single purchase and as high as $20,000.

After receiving the CSP card, you'd go about hitting that $4,000 minimum spend (MS). But maybe you only have enough expenses to put $1,000 on your card each month. In cases like this, we'd recommend purchasing gift cards you plan on using in the future. If you shop at Walmart, consider picking up a $500 gift card you can use throughout the year to help get you to meet the minimum spend requirement.

You'd also be surprised by how many of your recurring bills can be covered with a credit card. Utilities, cell phones and cable can usually be paid for with plastic. Even rent can be paid with a credit card (although services that allow you to pay rent with a card typically charge a fee, and we recommend avoiding paying any sort of fees for using a credit card. In cases like that, debit cards or ACH payments make more sense). After meeting that minimum spend requirement, Chase will deposit 50,000 ultimate rewards points to your account.

Great, so how much will this cost me?

How much have you paid for the 50,000 points? If you're paying your balance on time and in full each month, you shouldn't pay **anything**. While the CSP does have a $95 annual fee, it's waived the first year. So, you should be able to go about getting the bonus and cancelling or downgrading the card before your first annual fee is due. In this case, you really do get 50,000 points plus 4,000 points from your minimum spend (since you get at least one point for each dollar spent on the card) at no cost to you.

You might be thinking, "How can Chase hand out this many bonus points for free?" Well, most people don't pay their cards on time and in full each month; the interest and fees Chase gets from their average client is much greater than the value of 50,000 points. In our case, though, we're just going to be marked off as a loss on Chase's P&L report.

Let's go back to the bonus. What can 50,000 points get you? Here's a list:

- 10 Nights at an IHG PointBreaks hotel
- 6 Nights at a category 2 Marriott property
- 2 Round-trip domestic flights
- 2 Round-trip flights to Hawaii
- 2 Round-trip flights from the East Coast to Ireland
- 1 Business class flight from the East Coast to Ireland

Some of the above flights are valued at above $6,000. There is a teeny tiny caveat: you have to pay taxes on flights booked with miles, but it amounts to $6 for a domestic flight and is negligible in the grand scheme of things.

Let that settle for a moment. ***Signing up for a single card can get you two roundtrip flights from the east coast to Ireland for the cost of tax on the tickets.***

The Big Questions

Most people we've spoken with about travel hacking ask the same few questions after hearing about it for the first time, so we'll address them here.

Won't this impact my credit score?

Yes, but not in the way you think. The detriment to your credit score, when it comes to travel hacking, occurs when you open a new card or when you close an existing card. Whenever you open a new card, you get hit with a credit inquiry. This typically drops your credit score slightly, but only for a few months. Opening a card also lowers your average age of credit history, which will lower your credit score as well. When you close a credit card, you also get a temporary drop in your credit score. But for both opening and closing, the drop is relatively small, and your score usually goes back to what it was a few months later. However, the average age of credit history that goes down with each card opening does tend to lower your score more than the smaller impact of a credit inquiry.

But as you open *new* cards, your overall available credit continues to go up. And as your available credit goes up, the utilization of that credit should go down (ie, $3,000 balance on overall available credit of $20,000 represents a 15% utilization of credit. If you open a new card that doubles your overall available credit to $40,000, that $3,000 now is only a 7.5% utilization of credit). This impact has a positive effect on your credit.

And as long as you ***pay in full and on time*** for all of your credit cards, your credit score shouldn't be impacted greatly. Our credit scores have actually gone up since getting into travel hacking. That being said, if you plan on obtaining financing within the next year (say, for a mortgage), we'd recommend holding off on opening new cards until after you've secured the loan.

What are the limitations?

It depends on the financial institution. Chase has a famous "5/24" rule, meaning you cannot be approved for a new Chase card if you've opened five cards in the past 24 months. Because of this, travel hackers usually recommend you target Chase cards first, as they also tend to be the most lucrative and flexible. You can also re-sign up for a Chase bonus typically two years after you've opened the original card that contained the bonus. American Express only gives you the bonus once per lifetime for the specific card in question, so there certainly are limitations brand to brand. Some brands let you get the bonus as often as you'd like (assuming you've hit minimum spend, obtained the bonus and promptly canceled the card) with no waiting period. In all, these limitations can still allow you to accumulate a vast points balance in a relatively short amount of time, indefinitely. We tend to open a new card once every three months, which allows us to open a card, meet minimum spend and move on to the next card four times a year.

Between the two of us, we **could** get ten cards within 24 months and fall within Chase's 5/24 rule. And since we're usually only getting four cards per year, this allows us to use a revolving door system to reacquire bonuses every two years. Here's an example of what this look like in practice:

January 2015: Cody opens Chase Sapphire Reserve (bonus of 100,000 ultimate reward points)

April 2015: Georgi opens Chase Sapphire Reserve (bonus of 100,000 ultimate reward points)

July 2015: Cody opens Chase Sapphire Preferred (bonus of 50,000 ultimate reward points)

Oct 2015: Georgi opens Chase Sapphire Preferred (bonus of 50,000 ultimate reward points)

January 2016: Cody opens SW Rapid Rewards Premier card (bonus of 60,000 SW points) and closes or downgrades Chase Sapphire Reserve card from year prior to avoid annual fee

April 2016: Cody opens SW Rapid Rewards Plus card (bonus of 50,000 SW points) and Georgi closes or downgrades Chase Sapphire Reserve card from year prior to avoid annual fee

July 2016: Georgi opens Hyatt credit card (bonus of 40,000 Hyatt points and free night) and Cody cancels or downgrades Chase Sapphire Preferred card from year prior to avoid annual fee

October 2016: Georgi opens Marriott Rewards card (bonus of 75,000 points plus a free night) and Georgi cancels or downgrades Chase Sapphire Preferred card from year prior to avoid annual fee

January 2017: Cody can open the Chase Sapphire Reserve again for the current bonus

Within two years, these are the perks we earned from the above schedule:

- 300,000 Chase UR points
- 110,000 Southwest points, which qualifies us for the companion pass (discussed below)
- 40,000 Hyatt points and a free night
- 75,000 Marriott points and a free night
- $1,200 in travel credits from the CSR cards
- 2 Free Priority Pass Lounge cards, valid for two years
- Free Global Entry and through it, TSA Precheck

With these cards, we had to pay the following annual fees:

- $99 Annual fee for SW Premier
- $69 Annual fee for SW Plus
- $75 Annual fee for Hyatt
- $450 Annual fee for each CSR card

Yep, that $450 is a whopper of a fee. However, this particular card, at the time, granted a $300 per calendar year travel credit. So, we actually received $600 in travel credits each (we just bought SW gift cards and universal studios tickets through www.undercovertourist.com, which codes as travel), in addition to a Priority Pass lounge card for airport lounges and free Global Entry/TSA PreCheck certification, which grants access to expedited security and customs screening. In all, these benefits are a greater value than the cost of the annual fee.

Through all of this, we paid off our card balances in full and on time each month and beyond the annual fees, we were charged absolutely nothing. And since we can re-sign up for the bonuses two years later, we can just rinse and repeat this process. The game is constantly changing as devaluations come through (meaning points aren't worth as much as they were), bonuses change, and new policies go into place; but as long as you're nimble, you should be able to reap substantial benefits by pursuing travel hacking.

These points can add up to tens of thousands of dollars in value, depending on your redemption. Typically, a good redemption is $0.02/mile (i.e. $500 flight should be 25,000 miles), but for business and first-class redemptions, the redemption rate could be much higher.

And that Southwest Companion pass we earned? It allows us to have endless "buy one get one free" Southwest flights for the calendar year in which we obtained the pass and the following calendar year. You can earn the Companion Pass by obtaining 110,000 SW bonus points or by flying 100 qualifying one-way flights.

Of course, you're probably not going to fly 100 times in a year, so we'll focus on the points qualification. You can get 110,000 SW points by spending that much on their credit card, or you can simply open two of their three cards, making sure one has an elevated bonus of 60,000 points, to immediately cross the 110,000 mark. Once complete, you'll have 110,000 miles (plus 4,000 from meeting minimum spend on both cards) in addition to a free flight for your companion on every booking you make for essentially two years. SW often runs promos of one-way flights for $49 or 2,200 miles. This means you can get *51* one-way flights, in addition to *51* free companion flights from your companion pass and corresponding points. Opening two cards can score you ***over 100 flights!***

If you aren't willing to pay any annual fees, you can still pursue travel hacking. There are several cards that have either no annual fees or waive their initial account opening annual fee. As discussed above, the Chase Sapphire Preferred is one of these cards. As long as you cancel or downgrade before your one-year anniversary, you'll end up paying nothing, while collecting 50,000 ultimate reward points.

How can I use points to book different hotel brands and airlines?

This depends on the specific card you have. There are certain cards that only give miles for that program (Southwest cards will only give you Southwest points) and carry the risk of expiring if you don't use your points balance quickly enough (this is easily avoidable, though; simply log in to the portal of the rewards program in question and use some of your points to buy a small gift card when your expiration date is coming up). There are cards that act as "travel erasers" (these have minimal impact and we recommend avoiding them) and there are strict cash-back cards (again, minimal impact, so we recommend avoiding them). But the greatest cards are *transferable points* cards, because they allow you to book these different hotel brands and airlines. Chase Ultimate Rewards are a perfect example. The points you earn with them can be transferred to a plethora of partners for hotels or flights. You can also use the Chase portal to book travel directly with your ultimate rewards points at a discount, but usually, transferring to travel partners provides the biggest bang for your buck. Other transferable point programs include American Express Membership Rewards and Citibank ThankYou points. You can find more detailed information on how the booking and transfer process actual works on free sites dedicated to training people on how to use reward redemptions, such as TravelMiles101. Some services will even do it all for you for a small flat fee.

Travel miles can be very powerful if you target card-opening bonuses. The world of travel hacking can get pretty complex, but with discipline and thorough research, the rewards can be substantial. The only thing better than sipping a margarita on a golden beach is sipping a margarita on a golden beach for free.

Chapter 13

Which Investments?

If you've implemented even a few of our recommendations in this book so far, you have reduced your cost of living and now take home substantially more than you spend, and you've been using that surplus to aggressively pay off your debt. Whether you went with the mathematically superior "avalanche" method or the psychologically superior and our recommended "snowball" method, you're eventually going to reach the point where your consumer debt is totally wiped out.

Maybe you have a mortgage and maybe you even decided to keep some debt with an interest rate below 3%. Either way, your high interest debt (meaning all credit cards, high interest student loans, furniture payments and likely car loans) should now be completely gone.

Debt-Free Life is So Much Better

This chapter deals with where you should put your surplus now that it's not going toward debt. But first, a note on how life changes when you're debt-free.

Now that you've hit that final loan payoff button, rejoice. The feeling of being debt-free is a little like after you've been carrying a 50-pound backpack up a mountain, and at the top you can finally shrug it off and take in the majesty of nature. You feel lighter and a little less tightly wound. The air smells fresher. You have a new appreciation for the little things in life, like steak and lattes and $5 lipsticks and sunglasses that aren't from the dollar store.

Throw a party (we celebrated with family, barbequed ribs, and mimosas), and maybe loosen those expenses just a little. Once we hit the debt-freedom mark, we decided we'd get cable just during football season and reinstitute our gift-giving. After getting by on such a tight budget for so long, we felt like we were living the high-life. Burgers were a feast. A pay-per-view movie was a special treat.

The point is, life gets better. But the quickest way to lose that feeling is by reverting to the way you spent money before. So only increase or revive expenses that *genuinely* make you happy and that you truly believe are worth it. It's still wise to keep that Starbucks habit at bay. While we don't advocate living in a state of purposeful deprivation, the early retiree only spends money on things and experiences that are "worth it"—things that bring about lasting satisfaction.

Many people go out and replace their car every few years, even though they have a perfectly operating vehicle, because the initial dopamine rush from that original purchase eventually wears out. When you start to notice trends of purchases that give you that initial happy feeling that end up being short lived, stop making those purchases! This doesn't necessarily mean something that doesn't bring long-term satisfaction is something you shouldn't ever buy (that would mean we'd never eat at a restaurant again, and we do enjoy restaurants from time to time).

We all have different hobbies and passions. Maybe you do find great satisfaction by going through a morning "perfect cappuccino" routine for the rest of your life that requires a $500 espresso machine. Is that $500 spent going to lead to lasting life satisfaction for us? No. But if it does for you, that purchase would be worth it. The gist is this: once you've gotten yourself out of the hole you were digging, don't dig more holes! Even if they don't involve debt, because sometimes holes are just expensive habits. Shift your mindset to only purchase things you really need, or things that bring you long-lasting satisfaction. The things that don't fall into either of these categories should be rare enough to not lose their specialness, like eating out or buying a nice shirt. Should you follow this advice once you've finished paying off debt, you'll be able to shift that same surplus you were putting towards debt into something much more exciting: investments.

An Introduction to Investing

In previous generations, investing in stocks was quite the challenge. You had to pick winners and losers and you also had to time the market. You needed to guess when company A was going to have a good year and buy, and you had to guess when company B was about to have a bad year and sell. Or you diversified into multiple different asset-types and hoped they provided a positive return over the long run. If you didn't want to worry about all this work, you'd pick an investment firm who would do it for you and charge you a variety of fees, even during down years. Losing 4% on your portfolio in a year under the management of an investment firm that charged an assets-under-management (AUM) fee of 1% and put you in a mutual fund with an expense ratio of 1% meant you actually lost 6% that year.

Most investment firms are either privately owned or publicly owned by shareholders. In either situation, the owners of the company need to make a profit, but they also want to attract more investors to their company, so it's a balance between charging more for more profits and charging less to attract more clients. Today, when everything is said and done, these firms offer a variety of mutual funds to choose from that typically have an expense ratio (ER) of 0.51%[69] (that is, the percentage you're charged for the expense of operating the fund. In this case, for every $1,000 you have in your account, you'd be charged $5.10 at the end of the year). This has dropped significantly in recent decades; it was 0.95% on average in 1996 and even higher the further you go back. Add this to an investment advisor who charges an AUM fee of

---

[69] Sean Collins and James Duvall, "Trends in the Expenses and Fees of Funds, 2016" *ICI Research Perspective*, last modified May 2017, https://www.ici.org/pdf/per23-03.pdf

0.99%[70] (the fee charged for providing their services of guidance and advice), and you're looking at 1.50% in combined annual fees. This actual number looks better than it really is, as it's skewed by a firm called Vanguard. Since Vanguard has one in every five dollars in the mutual fund industry[71] along with their average expense ratio of 0.12%, the average ER is a lot higher if Vanguard isn't included in the average.

What is this firm with such a crazy low ER? In the 1970s, ultra-successful investor Jack Bogle recognized the problem of picking winners and losers and timing the market, so he created Vanguard, and through it, the first index fund. Index funds are a stroke of genius, as they simply track a segment of the stock market. For example, the fund Bogle created tracked the largest 500 companies in the nation, so when you buy this specific fund, you're buying a little piece of ownership of the largest 500 companies in America. This simplicity eliminated the need to pay someone to pick and choose winners, drastically reducing the cost of operating the fund.

The fund itself is decided on a regular basis, determined by which 500 companies are the biggest. And how has that fund performed since its inception in the mid-70s, through all of the crashes, stagflation, hyperinflation and wars? 11.11% per year![72] Taking inflation into account, the real return is closer to 7%.

That 0.39% (at least) difference between Vanguard and everyone else doesn't sound like much, but we'll get into just how big of a

[70] "2016 RIA Industry Study: Average Investment Advisory Fee is 0.99%", *RIA in a Box*, last modified December 8, 2016, http://www.riainabox.com/blog/2016-ria-industry-study-average-investment-advisory-fee-is-0-99-percent

[71] John Waggoner, "Vanguard's market share keeps growing" *InvestmentNews*, last modified December 12, 2016, http://www.investmentnews.com/article/20161212/FREE/161219995/vanguards-market-share-keeps-growing

[72] "Vanguard 500 Index Fund Investor Shares, *Vanguard*, last modified February 7, 2018, https://personal.vanguard.com/us/funds/snapshot?FundIntExt=INT&FundId=0040

difference this means for your portfolio growth later. Let's get into why Vanguard can charge so much less and still keep the doors open. We detailed above how most investment companies are owned privately or owned publicly. Vanguard, however, shifted all ownership of the company into the funds themselves. So, whoever owns Vanguard funds, in turn, owns Vanguard. Because of this, they have no traditional owner and can operate at cost. And because they can operate at cost, they can charge incredibly low fees, even down to 0.04% for a certain fund called VTSAX (Vanguard Total Stock Market Index Fund Admiral Shares).

The second reason they can keep their fees so much lower is the structure of the funds themselves. With most firms you have to hire a fund manager to pick and choose winners and you have to pay them handsomely for it. But most of the time, those managers can't even beat the baseline index (the performance of the stocks of the top 500 companies in the US). And by most of the time, we mean the *vast majority* of the time. Specifically, only *one in twenty* fund managers outperform the index.[73]

So, should you dump all your money into Vanguard's 500 Index Fund? Sure, you can do that.

We prefer the VTSAX though, because it doesn't just give you a little piece of ownership for the largest 500 companies in the US, but ownership of *every* publicly traded company in the U.S., big or small. Through this, you're basically betting on the U.S. economy. Although there are always going to be crashes and corrections, the market always recovers and grows. Sure, maybe everything will crash and burn and take decades to recover like the late-night gold-hawkers told us for years during the Great Recession, but at that

---

[73] Aye M. Soe and Ryan Poirier, "SPIVA U.S. Scorecard", *S&P Dow Jones Indices*, last modified December 15, 2016, https://us.spindices.com/documents/spiva/spiva-us-year-end-2016.pdf

point, it doesn't matter where you keep your money. Everyone will be screwed.[74]

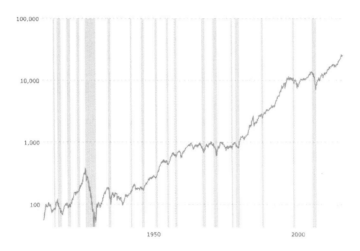

Though you'll hear panic during times of a long bull-run (sell before the drop comes!) and even more so when things start to drop (we're going back to zero!), as you can see, the market always goes up. It's a wild, bumpy ride, but if you're in it for the long run, you'll continue to see positive returns. Looking closely at the chart, you'll see a history of crashes and booms.

Because the market will always have both, people try to time the market (i.e., sell high and buy low.) The problem with this is that you must be right twice: you must correctly sell around when the market is at its top and then you have to promptly buy when the market is at its bottom. And for the rare times when someone has an accurate inkling for the top or bottom, they tend to get "one more day" syndrome. "Should I buy now if the economy's in the tank? What if we're in a bubble that's about to burst? What if it costs even less to get in tomorrow?" Before you know it, that

[74] "Dow Jones - 100 Year Historical Chart", *macrotrends,* last modified August 9, 2018, https://www.macrotrends.net/1319/dow-jones-100-year-historical-chart

person doesn't get in until prices are back to what they were pre-crash. On the flip side, someone might say during a crash, "Should I sell now or wait and see if tomorrow is the start of a recovery?" Before you know it, the floor opens up and they're left in the basement, kicking themselves.

You're probably wondering what you should do, then. Here's your answer: dump your money, as often and as much as you can, into VTSAX and *forget about it*, which is pretty much the strategy Warren Buffett recommends (though he recommends VFIAX instead, which tracks just the largest 500 U.S. companies and not all U.S. publicly traded companies).[75] You might be tempted to try and time the market, but it really doesn't work. We already showed that for people who spend their careers managing funds, only one in twenty beat the index. Along the same lines, Fidelity ran a study that confirmed that the accounts which performed best were owned by people who were...dead. The second best performing demographic? Those who forgot they had the account with Fidelity.[76]

The average investor loses money in the stock market because they try to dance in and out of it. Stick with what has proven to work and invest your surplus into low cost Vanguard Index Funds once you've eliminated your debt. Some people like having their money in a variety of different index funds: S&P 500, Total Stock Market, International Index, small-cap and mid-cap (referring to the level of market capitalization), but we tend to go with the simplicity of the VTSAX. It contains all small-cap, mid-cap and large-cap companies in the US, and because the bigger US companies already have a lot of international exposure (e.g. they sell iPhones in Europe, too), this fund should "cover" everything. And at an

---

75 Matthew Frankel, "Warren Buffett Just Revealed the Best Investment Most People Can Make", *The Motley Fool,* last modified February 26, 2017, https://www.fool.com/investing/2017/02/26/warren-buffett-just-revealed-the-best-investment-m.aspx

76 Tim Mcaleenan Jr., Fidelity's Best Investors are Dead", *The Conservative Income Investor,* last modified May 26, 2015, http://theconservativeincomeinvestor.com/2015/05/26/fidelitys-best-investors-are-dead/

expense ratio of 0.04%, you'll keep the vast majority of your returns (if you don't have $10,000 for an initial investment, the ticker will be VTSMX and will have a higher ER of 0.15%. It will, however, automatically convert to VTSAX and its lower 0.04% ER once you hit the $10,000 minimum).

The Staggering Impact of Fees

Through investing in index funds, not only will you end up performing at the same level of the top 5% of active fund managers, you'll save an incredible amount of money along the way. Say you go with a financial advisor that charges an AUM fee of 1%/year. This advisor then puts you in a mutual fund with an expense ratio of 1%. And let's say this financial advisor is so good at his job that he outperforms 95% of his colleagues, and thus matches the same returns you would've had if you had simply invested in index funds. He provides a real return of 7% on your investment. But after the 2% of fees are considered, your return is actually 5%. So, we're looking at a difference of 2%.

Doesn't sound like much, right? Well, let's look closer.

Say you saved up and invested $100,000 by the age of 30. From then on, you didn't touch the money or add to it. You just let it grow until you turned 65. In scenario 1, with the financial advisor and adjusted returns of 5% after inflation, you'd end up with $575,391.30.[77] Not too shabby.

Well, what if you just dumped that money into VTSAX and saved yourself 1.96%/year (1% for the advisor and .96% for the difference between VTSAX's 0.04% and the mutual fund's 1.00% expense ratio)? Overall, your return would be 6.96%, after inflation.

---

[77] "Compound Interest Calculator" *U.S. Securities and Exchange Commission*, last modified August 25, 2016, https://www.investor.gov/additional-resources/free-financial-planning-tools/compound-interest-calculator

Through this same time horizon, you'd be looking at $1,142,458.69.[78] *That 2% difference nearly doubled your return.*

As you can see, investment fees are huge when it comes to the impact they have on compound interest. And remember, this is amplified even further during down years, as you still have to pay that 2%. What if you lose 4% in the market that year? Well, you'll still get charged 1% from your financial advisor and 1% for the mutual fund fees, for a total loss of 6%.[79]

The Power of Compounding Interest

The above example doesn't just illustrate the power of low cost index funds—it also demonstrates the power of compounding interest. Typically, if people save $5,000/year, you'd assume that after 20 years, they'd have $100,000 in their account. If they put this in a no-return checking or savings account, this is true. But that $100,000 has a lot less buying power 20 years from now due to inflation.

If you earned simple interest on your money, it would cut down on the impact slightly as you gain a small percentage on your original contribution. But compound interest is where exponential growth occurs. Compound interest takes place when you invest your money into an asset that provides constant returns. Essentially, the money you invest generates more money, and that newly-generated money generates more money. If you invest $5000 and gain 7%, that $5,350 could generate another 7%, and that $5,724.50, which turns into $6,125.22, and so on. The more time

---

[78] "Compound Interest Calculator" *U.S. Securities and Exchange Commission*, last modified August 25, 2016, https://www.investor.gov/additional-resources/free-financial-planning-tools/compound-interest-calculator

[79] * That said, it may be wise to meet with a fee-only financial advisor to go through or formulate a plan on early retirement. Many advanced strategies presented in this book that a financial advisor should be able to help execute. Just make sure you pick one that charges a flat fee per appointment and not an asset-under-management fee.

you give it, the more money is generated, creating a very steep growth curve. When you look at compound interest returns, you don't see a straight upwards line. Instead you see a line that grows steeper and steeper the more time you give it. Just like this:

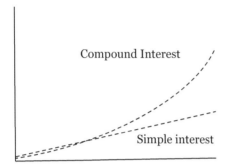

That's why you hear "your first million is the hardest to get." The more time and money involved, the bigger your returns will be. It's not uncommon to see millionaires get a higher return over one month than what their portfolios yielded over their first five years of accumulation.

That's the long and short of where you should put your money and why it works. In the next chapter, we'll look deeper into the difference between speculation and investment and how you can resist the temptation of "easy money" while still coming out on top.

Chapter 14

Don't speculate, invest!

We've established that if you send your money towards a low-cost index fund like the Vanguard 500 index fund (VFIAX) or the recommended Vanguard Total Stock Market Index Fund (VTSAX), you'll outperform 95% of active fund managers without paying the high costs of an actively managed mutual fund or a financial advisor.

These low-cost index funds are where you should be sending your money. We can debate whether it makes sense to include international index funds, small-cap index funds, mid-cap index funds and/or bond index funds, but regardless of what allocation you end up going with, if all or most of your money is in low-cost index funds, you should be set for the long haul.

But every once in a while, you'll see a stock, currency or opportunity pop up that seems too good to be true. As of this writing, that's bitcoin. A $100 investment in bitcoin on December 12, 2011 would've been worth $548,821 exactly six years later.[80]

Sounds sweet, doesn't it? But this kind of "investing" isn't investing at all. When you purchase an investment with a value based solely on selling it for more than you bought it for, that's speculating—or to put it more bluntly, gambling.

---

[80]"Bitcoin (USD) Price", *coindesk,* last modified February 20, 2018, https://www.coindesk.com/price/

The real story of bitcoin as an investment strategy, for many purchasers of the cyber currency, is not "get-rich quick," but "lose-your-money-like-you-spent-30-seconds-at -the-craps-table quick." Because six years and one month later on January 16, 2018, bitcoin had dropped from $19,000 to below $12,000. And six months after that? It dropped down to $6,000.

Georgi heard from one investor who bragged that he "got out at the right time" and made a killing, but that's precisely the point. How does one know when the "right time" is, especially if he isn't already an expert in cyber currency?

Speculators are those who try to "beat the market," as in beat the baseline index return (averaging 7%).
Investors are those who participate in the market.

An investor knows the market will have drops and peaks and is in it for the long run. Speculators try to make a quick buck by choosing a certain asset they believe can double or triple overnight. Sometimes speculators get lucky, but you don't want to bank your future on luck, do you? Remember how we said that most people lose money in the stock market? Speculation is the major reason why.

But you might protest, "You're just expecting the market to go up as a whole, isn't that just as 'speculative' as banking on Bitcoin?"

Let us further illustrate the difference.

Speculators try to time the market. You can do this with any stock, trying to buy low and sell high, and buy into other stocks that are "hot." Bitcoin is an especially pure sort of speculation, though. Without getting into too much detail, the technology behind Bitcoin isn't patented. Hundreds of cyber currencies are out there, made with the same Blockchain tech. What makes Bitcoin a speculative bubble is that its investors think *this* is the one that will take off and be increasingly used as a "real" currency (at best), and at worst, they just believe the value will go up enough for the prospect of a big payout to justify the risk of putting their money in it. There's no intrinsic value Bitcoin offers *over* the other cyber currencies, except the expectation that its value will grow. And its value grows because more people want to buy into it.

By contrast, when you buy into a total stock index fund, you essentially own a little piece of every publicly traded company. These stocks do fluctuate in price, but in the long term, they tend to reflect the actual success of that company. Those companies are successful because they are generating real goods and services in exchange for money. They actually *make money*. There are some, like Uber, who may not be making money (yet), but they are greatly outnumbered by the companies who do turn a profit. In essence, you've got the whole economy working for you, to make you money. There's real value behind your investment, where Bitcoin is mostly driven by people anticipating a higher price at which they can sell.

The high risk and volatility of speculative assets is not a good way to create and sustain wealth. Warren Buffet, the most successful investor of all time, evaluates companies by their "intrinsic value," not what their stock price is. The value an asset generates in actual dollars is what matters in the long run, and we are in it for the long run.

What about Real Estate?

There are other forms of investing that can provide greater returns than stocks. A very popular form is real estate. The greatest thing real estate has going for it is the power of *leverage*. You can put $40,000 down on a $200,000 house. If that house appreciates 5%, the home is now worth $210,000, providing you a 25% return on your investment ($10,000 return on your $40,000 down). This also has the opposite effect in that if it drops 5%, you have an even greater negative ROI on your leveraged money. Many "flippers" (teetering on the edge of speculation, these are people who buy homes at bargain prices, fix them up, and sell them typically within six months for a large profit) experienced this massive downside of leverage when the housing bubble burst in 2008.

But, on average, homes appreciate[81] and with leverage, this magnifies the power of your dollar. Smart investors typically only buy properties that will cash flow (that is, provide a real profit after all expenses are paid, including expenses like maintenance and vacancy) and at the same time, their renters are paying off the mortgage! So real estate has a beautiful quadruple effect of leverage, appreciation, principal payoff by renters, and cash flow.

It really can be a great wealth-builder. So, what keeps us from recommending this as the best way to pay for retirement? For one, it's not a passive investment type: as long as you're in the game, you're not really retired. Even if you hire out property management, you still have to find the deal and go about the paperwork to acquire the property. Then you have to manage your property manager and most likely have some sleepless nights over vacancies or major maintenance costs.

And although homes tend to appreciate, homes are illiquid, meaning they're much harder to sell than other assets like stocks.

Lastly, you must be good at it. You have to really know what the hell you're talking about. Many people have tried their hand at real estate investing, including flipping, and failed. They fail because they speculate and think prices will keep climbing up and up in a certain area, or they fail because they've misjudged the quality of their asset and/or the costs (time as well as money) one must sink into it before it gives a positive return.

So, if you think you might be good at real estate investing, you should give it serious research and consideration. However, the primary aim of this book is towards those who want investments that don't require much upkeep or, frankly, knowledge. Index

---

[81] "Historical Census of Housing Tables Home Values", *United States Census Bureau,* last modified June 6, 2021, https://www.census.gov/hhes/www/housing/census/historic/values.html

investing allows you to send all your money towards one or maybe a few different index funds and that's it. Real estate requires a lot more work, but like anything that requires additional effort, the returns can be worth it.

In either circumstance, you need to put your money into assets with real value.

Chapter 15

Finding Your Number

Now that you know which investment to target during the wealth building stage, we need to figure out how big your nest egg needs to be before you can officially declare your independence from the paycheck.

As discussed in the last couple chapters, we know that on average, index funds return roughly 7%, adjusted for inflation, per year. Some years they'll return 20% and some years they'll provide a negative return. But, overall, the stock market always goes up, even if it is a crazy, volatile ride. Now, "your number" (hereafter referred to as "your Number" or "the Number") needs to be large enough that you can safely withdraw a certain percentage of it without depleting your nest egg. If we know that stocks provide a real return (that is, adjusted for inflation) of 7% on average, you might guess that once your nest egg grows to a point where 7% of it matches your annual expenses, that you're there.

For example, let's say you have a nest egg of $600,000 and your annual expenses are $40,000. If the stock market provides a real return of 7%, $600,000 should crank out $42,000 per year, enough to cover your expenses forever. Sounds great. So, we're done, right?

Well, not quite. We're not considering two important risks. First is that, as we know, the market doesn't always provide a nice 7% return package every year. Although that's the average, some years will yield significantly less than that and some years will yield significantly more. Here's an example that shows this volatility, assuming the same $600,000 nest egg and $40,000 expense figure listed above.

Drawdown Example - $40,000 withdrawals (about 7% of nest egg in year 1)

Year	Balance	Withdrawal	Actual Real Return	Remaining Balance
1	$600,000.00	$40,000.00	-20%	$448,000.00
2	$448,000.00	$40,000.00	4%	$424,320.00
3	$424,320.00	$40,000.00	-8%	$353,574.40
4	$353,574.40	$40,000.00	0%	$313,574.40
5	$313,574.40	$40,000.00	10%	$300,931.84
6	$300,931.84	$40,000.00	8%	$281,806.39
7	$281,806.39	$40,000.00	2%	$246,642.51
8	$246,642.51	$40,000.00	0%	$206,642.51
9	$206,642.51	$40,000.00	4%	$173,308.22
10	$173,308.22	$40,000.00	0%	$133,308.22
11	$133,308.22	$40,000.00	25%	$116,635.27
12	$116,635.27	$40,000.00	20%	$91,962.32
13	$91,962.32	$40,000.00	25%	$64,952.90
14	$64,952.90	$40,000.00	18%	$29,444.43
15	$29,444.43	$40,000.00	18%	-$10,555.57

From the above chart, withdrawing 7% would lead to a complete loss of funds by year 15, even though the average return was 7%. A few underperforming years from the get-go led to total depletion. This is what's called *sequence-of-return risk*. Even though the

average returns are right around what we want to see, the returns
during the first few years—the most important years in one's
portfolio during the drawdown phase—were below average,
resulting in an uphill battle for the rest of this investor's life.

The second risk is, to quote every single fund provider's fine print,
"past performance does not guarantee future results." Even though
the past provides us with some very comforting data, which we'll
get into shortly, we still don't know what the future holds. As such,
we should lower our expectations to account for this risk.

The above example may have discouraged you a bit, but fear not! A
few professors from Trinity University encountered similar
concerns and built a study that would address this issue. The
results of the study were staggering and resulted in a well-used
phrase in the FIRE community: the 4% rule.

The Trinity Study

The Trinity Study used actual market returns for 30-year terms,
starting in 1926 (yes, this includes the Great Depression!) and
generated multiple "guinea pigs," each with their own nest egg,
based on various portfolio builds: 100% stocks, 75% stocks and
25% bonds, 50% stocks and 50% bonds, 25% stocks and 75%
bonds, and 0% stocks and 100% bonds.[82] They then made each of
these guinea pigs withdraw different percentages of their portfolio
annually, to see how many of them, if any, would still have a
positive balance after a 30 year drawdown period, and if so, how
much of a nest egg they'd have left. Keep in mind that they ran this
study based on inflation-adjusted withdrawals, which is what we'll
be using here. We'll use the most recent update to the study, which
covered data through 2009.

[82] Philip L. Cooley and Carl M. Hubbard and Daniel T. Walz, "Portfolio
Success Rates: Where to Draw the Line", *Financial Planning Association*,
last modified April 3, 2011,
https://www.onefpa.org/journal/Pages/Portfolio%20Success%20Rates%
20Where%20to%20Draw%20the%20Line.aspx

Although there were several fascinating results from this study, we will focus on a few:

1) Portfolio success rates for a withdrawal rate of 4%, based on a 75% stock and 25% bond allocation, were at 100%.

2) Portfolio success rates for a withdrawal rate of 4%, based on a 50% stock/50% bond allocation, were at 96%.

3) Portfolio success rates for a withdrawal rate of 4%, based on a 100% stock allocation, were at 98%.

These results are staggering. "But hold on," you might say, "that's great that the chances of success over 30 years are about as good as one can hope for, but if I retire at 30, I'd only be 60 by the time this 30-year window closed. What if there's not enough of a nest egg left to get me another 30 years?"

Well, the Trinity study went a step further and analyzed how much of a nest egg one would have left after the 30-year term. The results were based on an initial portfolio volume of $1,000, but since the early retiree will start with hundreds, perhaps thousands more than this, we'll adjust these balances to reflect an initial portfolio value of $600,000. Keep in mind that the below figures are adjusted for inflation, so the actual balances would be much higher than this:

1) Portfolio balance after 30 years of a withdrawal rate of 4%, based on a 75% stock and 25% bond allocation, would average *$3,580,800*.

2) Portfolio balance after 30 years of a withdrawal rate of 4%, based on a 50% stock and 50% bond allocation, would average *$1,782,600*.

3) Portfolio balance after 30 years of a withdrawal rate of 4%, based on a 100% stock allocation, would average *$6,045,000*.

Isn't that incredible? Even if you bumped withdrawal rates up to 7% post-inflation, based on a 100% stock allocation, you'd end with more money than you started with, on average.

So, what does this tell us? It means that 4% is about as safe as you can get. If you cut that down to 3-3.5%, the failure rate becomes nonexistent. Remember the chart posted above regarding a set withdrawal of $40,000? Here's an updated chart based on a 4% withdrawal rate of the original balance:

Drawdown Example - 4% Withdrawal Rate[83]

Year	Balance	Withdrawal	Actual Real Return	Remaining Balance
1	$600,000.00	$24,000.00	-20%	$460,800.00
2	$460,800.00	$24,000.00	4%	$454,272.00
3	$454,272.00	$24,000.00	-8%	$395,850.24
4	$395,850.24	$24,000.00	0%	$371,850.24
5	$371,850.24	$24,000.00	10%	$382,635.26
6	$382,635.26	$24,000.00	8%	$387,326.09
7	$387,326.09	$24,000.00	2%	$370,592.61
8	$370,592.61	$24,000.00	0%	$346,592.61
9	$346,592.61	$24,000.00	4%	$335,496.31
10	$335,496.31	$24,000.00	0%	$311,496.31
11	$311,496.31	$24,000.00	25%	$359,370.39
12	$359,370.39	$24,000.00	20%	$402,444.47
13	$402,444.47	$24,000.00	25%	$473,055.58
14	$473,055.58	$24,000.00	18%	$529,885.59
15	$529,885.59	$24,000.00	18%	$596,944.99

---

[83] Inflation is accounted for in the return rate instead of increasing the withdrawal amount to keep things as clear as possible.

After the same 15 years, you'd still have a remaining balance roughly the same as when you started. The above returns, which show a significant drop at the start of your drawdown period, represent a very unfortunate situation. Still, your balance should remain intact when using the 4% safe withdrawal rate, addressing a large area of concern that comes with sequence-of-return risk. And this is without utilizing some strategies we'll cover in later chapters that will hedge this risk even further.

Although past performance doesn't guarantee future results, it *is* the best indicator we've got. Though you could go with a higher 5% withdrawal rate which leads to success 82% of the time in a 75% stock and 25% bond allocation, we'll roll with a massive 20% withdrawal reduction to 4% to account for some of the risk.

Because of the "4% rule," calculating your number is a simple equation:

Simply take your annual projected retirement expenses and multiply them by 25.

If you plan to spend $20,000/year, your Number is $500,000. If you plan to spend $30,000/year, your Number is $750,000. Although these numbers may seem daunting, they can quickly be achieved through compounding interest and some strategies we'll mention shortly.

Before getting into these strategies, there are some details you need to consider. Most importantly, your Number shouldn't be based on your current expenses (although, the more you reduce those, the quicker you'll hit your number), but it should be based on your *projected post-retirement expenses*. You may be living on $40,000 now, but if you no longer need to work, maybe you can move somewhere that reduces your cost of living to $30,000, which would cut your number by 25%. On the other hand, if you want to retire in a more expensive area, you'll need to save more.

Obviously, you want this post-retirement expense figure to be as accurate as possible. Stabs in the dark just won't do when you're dealing with you and your family's welfare. With that said, there's much more to say on figuring out what you want your post retirement expenses to look like, which we'll cover in the next chapter.

Chapter 16

Adjusting Your Number for Post-Retirement Expenses

In chapter 1, we discussed the double effect of reducing an expense: It increases the surplus you have to reduce debt or increase investments, getting you to FIRE sooner, and it reduces the amount of money you need to reach FIRE, as you no longer have to sustain that expense.

But not all expenses can be reduced or eliminated during your working years. Maybe your high paying job forces you to live in a high-cost-of-living area and relocating to cut your expenses would hurt more than help, as you would no longer have that lucrative job. Although you can't take advantage of the double effect reducing a current expense has, if you eliminate or reduce an expense once you retire, it would at least produce the second effect.

In the previous chapter, we mentioned how you would need $1,000,000 saved to cover a lifestyle that accrues $40,000 of expenses each year. That figure is pretty intimidating, but if you reduce what you need to sustain yourself in retirement, that figure can shrink dramatically. Perhaps part of that $40,000 includes a rent payment of $2,000/month tied to living in a city. If you plan to move to a town that allows you to get the same square footage and amenities for $1,000/month, you'd then only need $28,000 to live on. Suddenly, your Number goes from $1,000,000 to $700,000, a *$300,000* decrease.

Let's discuss a few post-retirement expenses that can have a big impact on your Number, for better or worse:

Geoarbitrage

Geoarbitrage is essentially moving to a lower-cost-of-living area. We did this after Cody was able to secure a work from home position from his employer. No longer tied to Seattle's high cost of living, we were able to move to Central Washington and buy a home for a fraction of what a similar home would go for in Seattle.

But it's not so easy for most people to just pick up and move half a state away, especially if they're already well established in a regional company. If you're one of those individuals that can't move during the wealth-building stage, maybe you already have a place in mind you'd move to if you didn't have a job tied to where you live now—maybe closer to relatives or somewhere you've lived before or visited that you really fell for. If you don't know where you might move, there's no harm in doing some research and spending a vacation in a few prospective locations. Not only will a lower-cost-of-living area provide cheaper housing, but other budget line items, like groceries, utilities, childcare and other expenses tend to cost less in areas with lower housing costs.

Of course, if you're dead set on staying where you are, that's fine, too. You just might need to get a bit more creative or settle for a longer path to FIRE.

Healthcare

Healthcare is the single most hotly discussed topic in the FIRE community. Its future is murky at best, but it's hugely consequential to every single early retiree. Without a job, you will lose your health insurance benefits your employer likely provided and will now need to find a way to get coverage apart from an employer. As of the writing of this book, the Affordable Care Act is still largely intact, but the individual mandate penalty has been set to $0. This means you will no longer be penalized for not having health insurance, but we would **strongly** recommend having some sort of catastrophic coverage. You don't want to build up a retirement nest egg and then see it all disappear because you bet on your family's health.

As of now, there are two primary options available to the early retiree: health-shares and the Marketplace.

Health-share Ministries

Health-sharing ministries are a very intriguing option for the early retiree. It works similarly to a standard insurance program in that:

1) You pay a monthly "share," which acts as a premium.

2) You have an annual "unshared amount," which acts as an out of pocket maximum

3) You have a "personal responsibility per incident" total, which acts as a form of deductible (though some programs may waive this).

4) Depending on the program, you can get up to $1,000,000 per incident in coverage.

The share amounts range from $45-$224 for a single person per month, $90-$349 for a couple and $135-$499 for a family, based on the two most popular companies out there. The more your share is, the lower your personal responsibility per incident becomes and the higher your coverage per incident ends up being.

There are a few downsides though. First is that some health-shares have tables they utilize that have an expected cost for certain procedures and services. If they're billed above that amount, the difference can be billed directly to the individual. This doesn't happen too often; when it does, prices can be negotiated, but this is a potential concern.

Second, they don't take on individuals with pre-existing conditions if that person is currently undergoing treatment for that condition. If they're not undergoing treatment, health-sharing ministries occasionally take on individuals with pre-existing conditions for a higher share per month, but they *can* turn you down (health-share ministries are exempt from the Obama-era mandate of health insurance companies not being allowed to turn people away with pre-existing conditions).

Third, you must be a Christian to participate in health-sharing ministries and you must adhere to generally accepted Christian principles and beliefs: this means things like drug use or alcoholism will disqualify you from participation.

But if you are a Christian and you don't have an active pre-existing condition, joining a health-sharing ministry is a reasonably priced solution you should consider.

The Marketplace

But let's say you're not a Christian, you have a preexisting condition, or you think you can do better on the Marketplace. Well, this is the only other real option available. Those insane premium hikes over the 2010s weren't "fake news;" many people did in fact experience drastic increases in their premium costs. Several people in the FIRE community plan to pay between $10,000-$20,000 in annual premiums.

But these are people that have relatively high incomes. If you've implemented the cost-saving methods and strategies we've laid out, your post retirement expenses will likely be around $30,000/year if you're married. Even if they're not, let's go ahead and discuss what they should be to hit the sweet spot of Obamacare subsidies (yes, there's a sweet spot).

Before jumping in, a quick note on pursuing this: You may take some issue with adjusting your income (that is, what you pull out of your investment accounts) to get subsidies that are covered by other taxpayers, especially if you have a hefty asset balance. Why should full-time worker John cover health insurance costs of retired Jim with $700,000 in assets? We're not going to launch into a deep discussion on morality here. Some argue against it (for obvious reasons) and some argue that if certain legislators can't piece together a common-sense bill that has subsidy phase-outs instead of cliffs, that one should take advantage of it to show how broken the system really is.

We have eminently reasonable tax brackets that have steady increases for every dollar as they surpass thresholds. On the other hand, we have a health insurance program where a single additional dollar can result in *thousands of dollars* in lost subsidies/benefits. One can argue it should be changed, and perhaps people who can legally game the system shouldn't feel guilty about it. If you assume that everyone tries to reduce their tax bill, which often includes subsidies (that's what the refundable Child Tax Credit is, after all), is it really all that different to try to optimize insurance subsidies?

We urge you to draw your own conclusions. If you take a strong moral issue with this, feel free to skip the following information and pay full retail value, or go with a health-sharing ministry if you qualify.

The Marketplace uses your MAGI (Modified Adjusted Gross Income) when it comes to determining how much, if any, of a subsidy you'll get. MAGI is calculated as follows:

1) Add up all of your income for the year, *including* investment/retirement income.
2) Subtract educator expenses, HSA contributions, health insurance expenses (if you're self-employed), IRA deductions, alimony and student loan interest.

For the early retiree, you're no longer going to have HSA contributions or IRA contributions, and we'll assume you won't have any of the other line items you can subtract from gross income. So, your MAGI will effectively be all the income you live on, plus any other income gained from tax strategies (i.e. Roth conversion ladders and tax-gain harvesting, which we'll cover later).

Now that you've calculated your MAGI, let's take a look at how the plans work. The Marketplace operates on a four-tiered rating system of Platinum, Gold, Silver, and Bronze, which correspond to how much of your health care costs the plan will cover. Bronze is 60% and then it goes up 10% by each graduating plan, capping at 90% coverage for Platinum plans.

The subsidy you get is based on how close your MAGI is to the FPL (Federal Poverty Level) for your household size, as shown in the below chart. As long as your income falls within 400% of the FPL, you should qualify for a subsidy. If your income falls below 100-138% of the FPL, though, you'll likely be put on Medicaid. As you scale up the 200%, 300% and 400% poverty levels, your subsidy shrinks (but not too gradually, because the thresholds are still "cliffs.") As we said, there's a sweet spot: you get a "bonus" cost-sharing subsidy if your income falls within 139%-250% of the FPL.[84]

Annual 2018 Poverty Guidelines for the 48 Continental United States[85]

Family Size	100%	200%	300%	400%
1	$12,140.00	$24,280.00	$36,420.00	$48,560.00
2	$16,460.00	$32,920.00	$49,380.00	$65,840.00

[84] *President Trump removed these bonus subsidies in 2017, but based on current budget proposals, there's a very good chance these will be added back in by the end of 2018
[85] "U.S. Federal Poverty Guidelines Used to Determine Financial Eligibility for Certain Federal Programs", *U.S. Department of Health & Human Services,* last modified January 13, 2018, https://aspe.hhs.gov/poverty-guidelines

3	$20,780.00	$41,560.00	$62,340.00	$83,120.00
4	$25,100.00	$50,200.00	$75,300.00	$100,400.00
5	$29,420.00	$58,840.00	$88,260.00	$117,680.00
6	$33,740.00	$67,480.00	$101,220.00	$134,960.00
7	$38,060.00	$76,120.00	$114,180.00	$152,240.00
8	$42,380.00	$84,760.00	$127,140.00	$169,520.00
9	$46,700.00	$93,400.00	$140,100.00	$186,800.00
10	$51,020.00	$102,040.00	$153,060.00	$204,080.00
11	$55,340.00	$110,680.00	$166,020.00	$221,360.00
12	$59,660.00	$119,320.00	$178,980.00	$238,640.00
13	$63,980.00	$127,960.00	$191,940.00	$255,920.00
14	$68,300.00	$136,600.00	$204,900.00	$273,200.00

To recap:
1) You don't want income to be too low (<133% FPL), or else you'll be put on Medicaid.

2) You don't want income to be too high (>400% FPL), or else your subsidies will go away completely.

3) If you fall within 139%-250% of the FPL, you get bonus subsidies!

Annual 2018 Poverty Guidelines for the 48 Continental United States

Family Size	100%	200%	250%
1	$18,210.00	$24,280.00	$30,350.00
2	$24,690.00	$32,920.00	$41,150.00
3	$31,170.00	$41,560.00	$51,950.00

4	$37,650.00	$50,200.00	$62,750.00
5	$44,130.00	$58,840.00	$73,550.00
6	$50,610.00	$67,480.00	$84,350.00
7	$57,090.00	$76,120.00	$95,150.00
8	$63,570.00	$84,760.00	$105,950.00
9	$70,050.00	$93,400.00	$116,750.00
10	$76,530.00	$102,040.00	$127,550.00
11	$83,010.00	$110,680.00	$138,350.00
12	$89,490.00	$119,320.00	$149,150.00
13	$95,970.00	$127,960.00	$159,950.00
14	$102,450.00	$136,600.00	$170,750.00

If you keep your income under the above levels, you can qualify for some pretty big subsidies. We went to www.wahealthplanfinder.org and plugged in these very numbers for a family of three in our home state of Washington. Here are the results:

150% of FPL:

Out of Pocket Max: $1,850. Deductible: $1,850 for an individual and $3,700 for a family. Monthly Premium: **$97.29.**

200% of FPL:

Out of Pocket Max: $5,250. Deductible: $5,250 for an individual and $10,500 for a family. Monthly Premium: **$214.85.** (There are also options that raise the premium by $20-$30/month and reduce the deductible to $3,500 individual/$7,000 family.)

250% of FPL:

*Out of Pocket Max: $7,050. Deductible: $7,050 individual and $14,100 Family. Monthly Premium: **$349.87**.*

Those should look pretty similar to what you currently pay with your employer. For an early retiree, that's not too shabby.

As mentioned previously, if you implement some of the cost-cutting recommendations put forth earlier in this book, annual expenses of $30,000 for a family of three is completely doable during retirement. Based on the 250% FPL for a household size of three, this would give you over $20,000 more to work with during retirement after your living expenses, while still being able to qualify for substantial subsidies (we'll discuss how to use this additional room to minimize your tax bill in a later chapter).

If you're feeling a little overwhelmed, here's what you should remember if you pursue a Marketplace plan:

1) *Keep your income between 150-250% of the FPL* (based on the chart above)
   and,
2) *Never let your income go above 400% of the FPL*, or else you'll fall victim to huge premiums.

We've presented two solid options for healthcare, but this field is constantly changing. Because it can have a big impact on the early retiree, we'd strongly recommend keeping yourself apprised of the current political situation. It's possible Obamacare might not exist in two years. It's also possible we may be heading towards a single-payer system. Regardless, keep your eye on any regulatory changes to see how they'll impact your number.

College

Like healthcare, college is a hot topic in the FIRE community. College education has undergone insane hyperinflation over the past few decades.

For some perspective, according to the consumer price index,[86] a dozen large eggs costs $1.17 in December 1997. In December 2017, they cost $1.81, an increase of nearly 55% in 20 years. Milk went from $2.67 in December 1997 to $3.15 in December 2017, an 18% increase. Electricity went from $0.09 per kwh in December 1997 to $0.14 per kwh in December 2017, a 55% increase. And finally, gasoline went from $1.18 a gallon to $2.46, a 108% increase. So, over various industries and products, inflation has caused anywhere from a 50% increase over the past 20 years to a little over doubling their original costs.

Now, let's compare that to college.

In that same time span, private college tuition went from $16,233/year to $41,727/year, a *257% increase*.[87] Public out-of-state tuition went from $8,840/year to $26,010/year, a *294% increase*. Public in-state tuition went from $3,168/year to $10,691/year, a *337% increase*.

The average graduate in 2012 had $29,400 in debt,[88] and since student loans survive bankruptcy, this debt follows you to the grave.

So, 18-year olds are being offered bankruptcy-surviving debt for a service that has grown several factors of the inflation rate. If college prices continue to increase, we would not be surprised to

---

[86]"Databases, Tables & Calculators by Subject", *Bureau of Labor Statistics*, last modified February 7, 2018, https://data.bls.gov/cgi-bin/surveymost

[87]Briana Boyington, "See 20 Years of Tuition Growth at National Universities", *U.S. News & World Report*, last modified September 20, 2017, https://www.usnews.com/education/best-colleges/paying-for-college/articles/2017-09-20/see-20-years-of-tuition-growth-at-national-universities

[88]"Quick Facts about Student Debt", *The Institute for College Access & Success*", last modified March 2014, https://ticas.org/sites/default/files/pub_files/Debt_Facts_and_Sources.pdf

see college become obsolete, replaced by self-teaching, low-cost online "universities," tradeships and internships.

Personally, we don't plan on paying for our children's college education. We offer a couple reasons: First and most importantly, we don't believe a college degree is necessary to gain a good income in a likeable job—and we're pretty confident it will be even less relevant to employers 17 years from now.

Second, neither of us received assistance from our parents and we had to take out loans. The stakes were high; it was our own money (well, our Future Selves' money), so from the outset we took college pretty seriously and not as a 4-year, extra-boozy extension of high school. We made mistakes and got poor grades in some classes, yes, but they were our mistakes to make and no one else's. Should any of our children attend college, we would want them to have the same attitude toward the service they are paying for.

We'll let them know this well in advance, of course. The earlier our children get started working and saving, the more time compound interest will have to work its magic.

If you need a little help to see why this is a good parenting decision, consider this: $5,000 invested in your IRA each year during your twenties will produce $72,000 by age 30.[89] Then if you stop investing and just let that balance grow, by age 65, you'd have nearly $850,000.

Now let's say you go to college at 18 and by 22, graduate with some debt. You pay that off by age 25 and start investing $5,000 annually for the next ten years, and it grows to the same $72,000 by age 35. At this point, you've invested just as much. However, by age 65, your balance will be $591,000. That small 5-year window, when young adults are typically piddling away their income (and a

---

[89]"Compound Interest Calculator" *U.S. Securities and Exchange Commission*, last modified August 25, 2016, https://www.investor.gov/additional-resources/free-financial-planning-tools/compound-interest-calculator

good chunk of their student loans) on kegs, lattes, leggings and rideshare trips, resulted in *a difference of over a quarter million.*

Nevertheless, college is a deeply personal decision for parents and students, so we're here to provide some hacks should you decide to pay for your child's college education.

Hack #1: A 529 plan

This plan, while not tax deductible, allows you to contribute to an account that then grows tax free. So, you pay taxes on the contributions, but whatever gains your child takes out will be tax free. This was made even sweeter with the recently passed Tax Cuts and Jobs Act, which gives you the option to use those funds on qualifying private and homeschool expenses for the pre-college years. So, if you were to contribute $200/month to this plan starting when your child is born, it should grow to about $90,000 by the time they're 18.[90] We'd say this should cover college, but as we've detailed above, college costs don't increase with the standard inflation rate. It may be $100,000/year 20 years from now. That brings us to hack 2.

Hack #2: Dual enrollment

Washington state currently has a program called "Running Start." Other states have similar programs, or at least programs for earning college credit in high school, like AP. Students gain entry to the Running Start program specifically after passing a couple tests to place into college level Math and English classes. If they score high enough, they can attend community college in lieu of their junior and/or senior year of high school, tuition-free. They still pay for books, but these shouldn't be more than $1,000/year (they could be much less, if you're good at hunting deals). This allows you to graduate high school with an associate's degree that

---

[90] "Compound Interest Calculator" *U.S. Securities and Exchange Commission*, last modified August 25, 2016, https://www.investor.gov/additional-resources/free-financial-planning-tools/compound-interest-calculator

should be transferable to most public 4-year colleges. So instead of needing to pay for four years of college, you only need to pay for two. When combined with a 529 balance of $90,000, this *should* cover all college expenses.

Hack #3: Scholarships

There's much to say about scholarships, but first you need to know why your high school student needs to hunt them down like it's their full-time job. Cody breezed through high school and Running Start, graduating two years early with a high school diploma and an A.A. degree and a stellar GPA. When applying for University to get his B.A., he didn't qualify for any scholarships (it turns out it's hard to find scholarships for middle class white males), but he figured he could qualify for some grants, so he completed the FAFSA. The FAFSA is a financial aid form that a student has to complete each year of college. It uses your income and assets, but most importantly, it looks at your parents' income and assets to determine your EFC, or expected family contribution. There is a way to be treated as an independent on the FAFSA, so your parents' income and assets aren't included, but you have to be either 24 or married—requirements most recent high school graduates don't meet. This EFC is the annual number the federal government believes you'll get from your parents each year for college expenses. And while Cody's parents didn't have much in the form of assets, they did have a relatively high income at the time, which means his EFC was at the top end of the scale.

What did this mean? It meant he didn't get any grants, as the federal government assumed his parents would cough up $20,000+ each year to pay for his college. How much did his parents *actually* give? $0. So, Cody figured loans were his last and only option. As it turns out, though, even that was wishful thinking. With such a high EFC, ***he couldn't even qualify for student loans***. He managed to get his parents to sign up for a Parent Plus loan at a very high interest rate, a loan he promised he would pay off (which we did).

So, you and/or your children should apply for as many scholarships as possible. But be warned: even if you set yourself up to succeed as much as you possibly can, you might find out you don't even qualify for student loans, let alone grants or scholarships.

Hack #4: The FAFSA

There's good news for youngsters of early retirees who might have a hard time finding scholarships: the FAFSA can be "hacked[91]." This is a method which offers the possibility that neither you nor your children will need to pay anything out of pocket for college. Similar to health insurance subsidies, you'll need to decide if you feel comfortable taking advantage of grants by adjusting your income. We discussed that in the vast majority of situations, the parents' income/assets are taken into account when determining the EFC. For the early retiree with children approaching college age, your spending likely isn't very high. As discussed before, most households who act on all of the cost-cutting strategies and methods listed in this book should be able to keep their annual expenses around $30,000. But since the EFC calculation is based on assets also, which early retirees have a lot of, your assets will likely quash you or your children's potential to qualify for grants, even if your post-retirement income is close to the Federal Poverty Line.

This is where the "simplified FAFSA" comes in. If you qualify for the simplified FAFSA, only your income is considered, **not your assets**.[92] This changes everything. So how do you qualify for this simplified FAFSA? You must meet the following two requirements:[93]

---

[91] "How a Millionaire Retiree Could Get as Much Aid for College as Someone Who's Broke", *Seonwoo's Musings,* last modified April 29, 2017, https://seonwoolee.com/fafsa-auto-zero-efc/
[92] "Simplified Needs Test and Auto-Zero EFC", *Edvisors,* last modified January 11, 2014, https://www.edvisors.com/fafsa/eligibility/simplified-needs-test/
[93] There are more ways than this, but they require participation in government aid programs. So, for purposes of this book, we will not discuss them here.

1) You must file either a 1040A or 1040EZ return

2) You must keep your AGI below $50,000

Let's start with the first requirement. The 1040A or 1040EZ are two of the three types of tax return forms. The other is the 1040. If you have to complete the 1040, you are immediately disqualified from the simplified FAFSA. So, what would be helpful here is what you should **not** be doing to stay qualified for the simplified FAFSA. Doing any of the following things will require a 1040, which means you're disqualified:

1) **Itemizing:** With the Tax Cuts and Jobs Act, the standard deduction for a married couple filing jointly is doubling to $24,000. This means a lot less people will be itemizing and will instead be taking the standard deduction, which is exactly what you'll need to do if you want to qualify for the simplified FAFSA.

2) **Having Self-Employment Income**: If you're self-employed post-retirement, unfortunately there's not much you can do here, unless you decide to take a hiatus while you or your children are in college.

3) **Having Capital Gains and Losses:** We'll discuss how to do both things in a later chapter, but keep in mind that once you learn how, you'll want to avoid going through the capital gains/loss harvesting process while you or your children are in college to avoid triggering the 1040.

4) **Having Rental Income:** This is another advantage for passive index investors over real estate investors. If you decide to go the rental route to get to financial independence, just be wary that this will kill your ability to hack the FAFSA.

5) **Taking the Foreign Tax Credit:** This book advocates holding everything in a combo of a total stock market index

fund or a total bond market index fund, so you shouldn't have anything in international funds (even though the total stock market fund does have international exposure). If you do, just sell all your international holdings while you/your kids are in college, so you can still hack the FAFSA.

6) **Itemizing the year prior:** This is important. If you normally itemize, you need to start to prepare for FAFSA-hacking a year before your kids go to college. Maybe even two years to create a safety net.

7) **Logging HSA contributions and/or HSA distributions:** We're a big fan of the HSA, but you'll need to avoid reimbursing yourself for medical expenses using your HSA account (we'll discuss this in depth in a later chapter) during the years you or your kids are in school. But don't be too worried here; as long as you keep your receipts, you can reimburse yourself for past expenses once your kids are out of college.

8) **Taking the Alimony Deduction**: As long as you don't do any of these eight items, you should just need to file a 1040A or 1040EZ at the end of the year, which will allow you to meet requirement #1 of FAFSA hacking.

As for requirement 2, you need to keep your income below $50,000. If you do that, only your income will be taken into account when calculating the EFC. Better yet, if you keep your income below $25,000, you *automatically qualify for a $0 EFC*. This is what we're targeting. If your expenses are more than $25,000, Roth IRA and Roth 401k distributions aren't included in your AGI calculation. We'll discuss the Roth conversion ladder in a later chapter, but at this point, just know that you can pull more than $25,000 during these years, but the extra funds will just need to come from your Roth accounts (or you can pull investments a year or two before you/your kids go to college so you have a cash buffer built up to cover expenses beyond $25,000).

To recap: *Make sure you qualify for form 1040A or 1040EZ and keep your post-retirement income below $50,000, with the sweet spot being below $25,000*, and you should see several grants coming your way.

Making college affordable just takes some discipline and planning. A combo of FAFSA hacking, scholarships, 529 investments, dual-credit classes in high school and some part time work in college should get you or your kids to a degree with little to no student loans.

Mortgage

So far, we've covered two areas that are hotly debated and discussed in the FIRE community: healthcare and college. We'll finish the discussion with the third major factor impacting your Number: housing costs.

As we discussed in Chapter 6, "Rent vs. Buy" is a hotly debated question in the FIRE community. Countless studies, articles and books have been published on this topic, and there's merit on both sides of the argument. But let's do a little recap here: If you live in a high-cost-of-living area where you can rent a home for $2,500 a month or buy an equivalent home for $750,000 (which would result in a $3,000+ mortgage payment), it probably makes sense to rent.

However, if you live in a low cost of living area where you can find a decent home under $300,000, it probably makes sense to buy, as eventually your mortgage-free home will only require property tax, insurance, and maintenance expenses—things that add up to a fraction of what the going rent is in your area.

The debate gets more complicated when other factors are discussed, namely:

1) Whether or not you "buy up" when purchasing a home in preparation for the future. If you buy a bigger house than you

need now to prep for growing your family later, you pay more over the person who rents based on current needs.

2) Whether the down payment you need for your house would've had greater returns in an index fund compounded over the same 30-year term as your mortgage.

3) The inflation hedge a home provides (20 years from now, a gallon of milk might double in price, but your fixed mortgage payment won't change. Although property tax and insurance will likely keep up with inflation, those only represent a fraction of your monthly payment).

4) Various loan programs that require little to no money down, which home buyer proponents argue counter the second factor mentioned above.

This discussion could get pretty far into the weeds, so for our purposes we'll focus this section to benefit those who have already made the decision to buy, or to those who plan to buy post-retirement (maybe you live in an area where buying doesn't make sense now, but after retiring, you can move to an area with a lower cost of living, thus allowing you to buy then).

Now, your mortgage's impact on your Number is two-fold:

1) *Assuming* you have a fixed-mortgage or plan on getting one, it will not be impacted by inflation, thus serving as a hedge.

2) Eventually, your mortgage will be paid off, allowing you to reduce your annual expenses, in turn resulting in needing a smaller nest egg for retirement.

This is where the math starts to get tricky, so bear with us. From chapter 15, we know the following based on the results of the Trinity study:

1) Portfolio success rates for a withdrawal rate of 4%, based on a 75% stock and 25% bond allocation, were at 100%.

2) Portfolio success rates for a withdrawal rate of 4%, based on a 50% stock/50% bond allocation, were at 96%.

3) Portfolio success rates for a withdrawal rate of 4%, based on a 100% stock allocation, were at 98%.

If we look at success rates for portfolios that aren't adjusted for inflation, this is what we get from the same Trinity study:[94]

1) Portfolio success rates for a withdrawal rate of 6%, based on a 75% stock and 25% bond allocation, were at 96%.

2) Portfolio success rates for a withdrawal rate of 6%, based on a 50% stock/50% bond allocation, were at 98%.

3) Portfolio success rates for a withdrawal rate of 6%, based on a 100% stock allocation, were at 93%.

As we can see, if all of your expenses didn't rise with inflation, you'd be able to maintain a 6% SWR. But as we know, overall living costs tend to increase over time. If you have a fixed mortgage, however, your principal+interest payments will never change. This means that *as a homeowner, you can effectively raise your safe withdrawal rate without raising your risk.*

To find out how much you can raise your SWR, add up all your projected post-retirement expenses. You'll want to keep the rest of this chapter in mind when projecting these out, but here's an example:

94 Philip L. Cooley and Carl M. Hubbard and Daniel T. Walz, "Portfolio Success Rates: Where to Draw the Line", *Financial Planning Association*, last modified April 3, 2011, https://www.onefpa.org/journal/Pages/Portfolio%20Success%20Rates%20Where%20to%20Draw%20the%20Line.aspx

Sample Monthly Expenses for a family of 4

Mortgage: $1,200 ($300 goes to property tax/insurance, $900 goes to principal and interest)
Utilities: $200
Cell Phone: $80
Healthcare: $360
Groceries and Personal Care: $500
Gifts/Travel: $100
Gas & Auto Maintenance: $100
Home Maintenance: $100
Kids' Programs: $100
Total Expenses: $2,740

In this scenario, your total expenses are $2,740/month or $32,880/year. Based on the standard SWR calculation, we know you must save up 25x these expenses, or $822,000, before you have a large enough nest egg to be considered financially independent. However, of the $2,740 in monthly expenses, the $900 that goes towards principal and interest isn't impacted by inflation, and that's 33% of your budget.

Because of this, we can increase your SWR and lower your FIRE number. Using the same example above, this is what that would look like:

Inflation-Protected Expenses (aka principal and interest payment): 33%
Inflation-Impacted Expenses: 67%

Adjusted SWR:
SWR: 6% for 33% of your expenses (since you don't have to account for inflation)
SWR: 4% for 67% of your expenses
Adjusted overall SWR: 4.66% (33% of 6%+67% of 4%)

This drops your Number from \$822,000 to \$705,580.[95]

Our hope is that the Number you calculated out for yourself or your family in the last chapter is a bit smaller after factoring in the contents of this chapter. After hacking your cost of living expenses, college savings, healthcare expenses and safe withdrawal rate, your refined Number should look a little less intimidating.

---

[95] * Astute readers will notice that this calculation has one problem: as inflation increases your non-principal+interest expenses year after year, your principal+interest payment represents less and less of your annual expenses, as a percentage. For example, if during year 1, your fixed interest+principal payments represent \$1,000 of your \$4,000 expenses or 25% and five years later, your \$3,000 of other expenses have risen with inflation to total \$3,500, your fixed \$1,000 payment now only represents 22% of your total annual expenses. While you can update the Adjusted SWR each year to account for this, we hold that your eventual mortgage payoff cancels out this impact.

Chapter 17

Sequence-of-Return Risk

We just discussed how owning a home can have a positive impact on your FIRE journey, but there is yet another perk to home ownership. In addition to your increased safe withdrawal rate, eventually you'll pay off your mortgage.

In today's environment of low interest rates typically under 4%, it mathematically doesn't make sense to pay off your mortgage early. Why drop $200,000 to pay off your 4% mortgage when you can drop $200,000 in index funds, where average returns are above 7% after inflation? One reason is it simply feels good to own your home outright, and we'll get into the other reason shortly. But choosing either investment or mortgage payoff for your money is leagues better than what the average person is doing.

Regardless of whether you pay your mortgage off early, you will eventually pay it off (unless you keep moving to increasingly more expensive houses and never make any progress on your mortgage). A lot of people in the FIRE community will treat this massive expense-reducing event as icing on the cake and will not adjust their withdrawal rate accordingly. In reality, there isn't really a good way to account for the eventual mortgage payoff if you decide not to pay it off before FIRE. As we just mentioned, paying off your mortgage early doesn't financially make sense if you look at it from a raw numbers perspective, but this book isn't a book on how to maximize investment returns, but rather about how to achieve FIRE and sustain your nest egg by mitigating risk. So for purposes of our message, paying off the mortgage early is encouraged for one overwhelming reason: sequence-of-return risk.

Sequence-of-Return Risk

You'll recall from chapter 15 that sequence-of-return risk is the risk to your portfolio based on market returns. If returns in the first few years are very low, this could wipe out your nest egg very quickly. If they are high, you'll have even more flexibility with how much you can withdraw. A risk as big as this (in terms of what it can do to your investments, not the likelihood of it happening) must be covered in depth.

Sequence-of-return risk (SRR) is the single most daunting roadblock to sustaining and growing your nest egg once you pull the trigger on FI. Even though the stock market has returned 7% on average, as you know, that number isn't a nice, neat package every year. Some years it might jump 20% and some years it might drop 40%. The early retiree wants those major drops to happen either during the early stages of the wealth-building stage or *after* the first ten years of retirement, since major drops during the latter portion of wealth-building phase, or right after you pull the trigger on early retirement, can devastate your nest egg.

For example, let's say your annual expenses are $40,000. This means you need a cool $1,000,000 to retire. However, let's also assume you have a mortgage and your principal+interest equates to 30% of your expenses. Using the formula in the last chapter, your adjusted safe withdrawal rate would be (30% of 6%+70% of 4%) 4.60%, meaning your number to achieve FIRE is actually $870,000. We'll run through three examples of what your returns over the first ten years may look like, starting with the historical average of 10% returns and using an inflation rate of 2%. Keep in mind that the $12,000 of expenses that cover your principal and interest payments will not increase with the 2% inflation rate, as that's a fixed payment.

Yr.	Starting Balance	Withdrawal Amount	Remaining Balance	Interest Rate	Year-End Balance
1	870,000.00	40,000.00	830,000.00	10%	913,000.00
2	913,000.00	40,560.00	872,440.00	10%	959,684.00
3	959,684.00	41,131.20	918,552.80	10%	1,010,408.08
4	1,010,408.08	41,713.82	968,694.26	10%	1,065,563.68
5	1,065,563.68	42,308.10	1,023,255.58	10%	1,125,581.14
6	1,125,581.14	42,914.26	1,082,666.88	10%	1,190,933.56
7	1,190,933.56	43,532.55	1,147,401.02	10%	1,262,141.12
8	1,262,141.12	44,163.20	1,217,977.92	10%	1,339,775.71
9	1,339,775.71	44,806.46	1,294,969.25	10%	1,424,466.17
10	1,424,466.17	45,462.59	1,379,003.58	10%	1,516,903.94

You're looking great after ten years. To be fair, the $1,516,903.68 would be worth $1,307,748.04 of today's dollars due to inflation, but that figure still represents a 50.5% increase from your starting balance. Not only were you able to sustain your nest egg, it grew substantially!

Next, we'll go with standard returns up until year 10 where we'll see a 30% drop:

Year	Starting Balance	Withdrawal Amount	Remaining Balance	Interest Rate	Year-End Balance
1	870,000.00	40,000.00	830,000.00	10%	913,000.00
2	913,000.00	40,560.00	872,440.00	10%	959,684.00
3	959,684.00	41,131.20	918,552.80	10%	1,010,408.08
4	1,010,408.08	41,713.82	968,694.26	10%	1,065,563.68
5	1,065,563.68	42,308.10	1,023,255.58	10%	1,125,581.14
6	1,125,581.14	42,914.26	1,082,666.88	10%	1,190,933.56

7	1,190,933.56	43,532.55	1,147,401.02	10%	1,262,141.12
8	1,262,141.12	44,163.20	1,217,977.92	10%	1,339,775.71
9	1,339,775.71	44,806.46	1,294,969.25	10%	1,424,466.17
10	1,424,466.17	45,462.59	1,379,003.58	-30%	965,302.51

Although the portfolio took a pretty big hit, your ending balance is still in pretty good condition. After inflation, you'd have the equivalent of $833,476.02 in today's dollars, but those dollars should have greater purchasing power, as crashes typically deflate prices of goods and services across the board.

Lastly, we'll go with a 50% drop right off the bat, followed by 12% annual increases every year after:

Year	Starting Balance	Withdrawal Amount	Remaining Balance	Interest Rate	Year-End Balance
1	870,000.00	40,000.00	830,000.00	-50%	415,000.25
2	415,000.25	40,560.00	374,440.25	12%	419,373.08
3	419,373.08	41,131.20	378,241.88	12%	423,630.91
4	423,630.91	41,713.82	381,917.08	12%	427,747.13
5	427,747.13	42,308.10	385,439.03	12%	431,691.71
6	431,691.71	42,914.26	388,777.45	12%	435,430.75
7	435,430.75	43,532.55	391,898.20	12%	438,925.98
8	438,925.98	44,163.20	394,762.78	12%	442,134.32
9	442,134.32	44,806.46	397,327.86	12%	445,007.20
10	445,007.20	45,462.59	399,544.61	12%	447,489.96

This scenario is a lot scarier. You may have spent over a decade building up a nest egg of $870,000 to retire, only to see it be halved immediately following retirement. Although average returns are 10% before inflation, the most important returns are for the first few years of your retirement.

If returns are average or above average for the first ten years or so, your investments would have gained so much traction that a crash would bring you back down to your starting balance, at worst. And your starting balance at that point would have so much more power. Why? Well, there are two reasons: first, deflated prices usually follow a crash, meaning your dollar will go further. Second, a crash is usually followed by a strong bull market that will grow your nest egg quickly.

However, if you experience the crash immediately following your retirement, it may be difficult to sustain your expenses forever. So, what can we do to avoid or mitigate this major risk to our portfolios? The answer is three-fold:

1) **Be flexible**. Although the 4% rule leads to a solid success rate, you shouldn't just pull 4% every year without regard to economic circumstances. You should always keep an eye on the market. This doesn't mean you have to check it every day and panic when corrections come through. It simply means that in down years, maybe take a little less than 4%, perhaps 3-3.5%. The same goes for up years. If you have periods of 30% jumps in your net worth in a single year, sure, go ahead and take out 5%. This is why it helps to err on the side of caution when projecting your post retirement expenses. Not sure if you need $5,000/year for groceries or $7,000? Go with the $7,000 figure and during down years, try to spend closer to the $5,000/year mark. Maybe create some additional income during down years through side gigs. Or perhaps you can go on a cheaper family vacation that year and make up for it in boom years. The point is this: try to be flexible depending on market returns, *especially* during your first few years of retirement, and you should be able to mitigate a lot of the risk to your welfare, if not your portfolio.

2) **Let the 4% rule reign supreme.** According to the Trinity Study, you can withdraw 5% after inflation and still be successful 82% of the time. In fact, there are some 30-year periods in which you could've withdrawn over 7%, after inflation, and still ended up with more than you started.[96] We go with 4% (and some proponents even argue for 3.25%), even though you still have a solid chance of success at 5%, to account for sequence-of-return risk. Reducing the safe withdrawal rate to 4% holds up a portfolio in cases where a retiree hits his number, quits work and sees a market crash immediately following. The 4% rule is a tall hedge against SRR.

3) **Paying off the mortgage early**. We teased this earlier in the chapter and now we can discuss it in some more depth. When you have a mortgage, it likely is your biggest line item expense post-retirement. During your early years of retirement, you're selling a lot of your shares to cover this large expense. While this isn't a big deal, if the market takes a hit right off the bat or underperforms during your first few years of retirement, you'd end up withdrawing to pay for your mortgage during a time when those shares are "on sale"—effectively selling low to cover your fixed mortgage payment. Additionally, having a mortgage takes away some of your flexibility, our first hedge against sequence-of-return risk.

Let's run with two examples to illustrate this further. In situation A, John has a mortgage with a principal+interest payment of $1,000. His expenses, including this mortgage, are $4,000/month. In situation B, Jennifer has no mortgage and as such, has expenses of $3,000/month. If the market gets cut in half and each respond by cutting their withdrawals in half, John takes out $2,000/month, but since his mortgage accounts for $1,000, he's only left with $1,000 to spend on non-mortgage expenses. Jennifer, however,

96 Philip L. Cooley and Carl M. Hubbard and Daniel T. Walz, "Portfolio Success Rates: Where to Draw the Line", *Financial Planning Association*, last modified April 3, 2011, https://www.onefpa.org/journal/Pages/Portfolio%20Success%20Rates%20Where%20to%20Draw%20the%20Line.aspx

has $1,500 to spend on non-mortgage expenses, so her discretionary spending is 50% more than John's.

Although the mortgage provides a hedge against inflation, during times of deflation, a mortgage can be seriously restrictive. Your $1,000 mortgage payment might look great ten years from now when the price of milk has doubled, but if you pull the trigger on retirement and the market crashes and milk is now half of what it cost a year ago, that $1,000 mortgage payment feels like a $2,000 mortgage payment. Paying off the mortgage early is also more appealing than ever with the recently passed Tax Cuts and Jobs Act. With the standard deduction now doubled and with reductions in the SALT deduction, the standard deduction will make more sense than itemizing, which means the argument that you should have a mortgage to write off interest and reduce your tax bill is becoming less and less applicable.

To sum it up, sequence-of-return risk is a very real threat during the early retiree's first few years. If you remain flexible, though, abiding by the 4% rule (or less during down years) and paying off the mortgage, you can mitigate a lot of the risk.

Chapter 18

Pre-Tax Buckets

The last few chapters have covered what investments you should go with, finding your FIRE Number, adjusting your Number for post-retirement expenses, and how to combat sequence-of-return risk. At this point, you should feel comfortable on what your Number looks like and what to invest in to get there.

We like to think of this journey as a road trip. First, you need to decide where you're going—that's your Number. Next, you need to decide which fuel your car needs to get you there—we've made a pretty good case, we think, that this should be VTSAX. Third, you need to hit the road and accelerate. Pushing down on the gas pedal here represents compound interest. The more money you put into investments, the more money it creates and, in turn, the money your money created creates more money. It's like a snowball collecting more and more snow until it becomes a massive unstoppable force. These three things: your destination, your fuel, and stepping on the pedal will get you to your Number quickly.

You know what will get you there even faster, though? Nitrous oxide. Maybe you've seen it in a *Fast and Furious* movie. Paul Walker (may he rest in peace) pushes a button and the car accelerates so quickly that it slams him back into his seat. As it relates to financial independence, certain pre-retirement investment vehicles act like nitrous oxide.

We're going to mix metaphors a bit here because we often refer to these vehicles as "buckets," but just roll with it. Just picture them as buckets packed with nitrous oxide canisters.

We've discussed what investments you should go with and why. This typically entails opening a brokerage account with Vanguard and dumping as much money as you can into the Vanguard Total Stock Market Index Fund. But unfortunately, you are contributing post-tax dollars. This means that if you fall into the 25% tax bracket, you must make $1.25 for every $1.00 you contribute to your taxable brokerage account. And although you can still get to FIRE quickly, it will take some additional time and effort to cover taxes along the way. This is where tax-deferred investment vehicles, or "pre-tax buckets," come in:

- **401K:** If you're employed, chances are you have access to one of these.

- **457:** If you work for a non-profit, you'll have something similar to a 401k called a 457 and if you work for the government (like a public-school teacher), you'll have access to a 403(b) plan *in addition* to a 457 plan. These plans allow you to contribute $18,500 (as of 2018, more if you're older than 50) pretax dollars to them, in addition to the likely employer match you'll realize by contributing (usually between 3-6%).

- **Solo-K:** If you are self-employed, you can set up your own 401k, often dubbed "Solo-K."

- **Pre-max IRA:** In addition to the work-sponsored plans, everyone can contribute $5,500 per year tax-free to a personal retirement account called an IRA. There are some income restrictions, but this vehicle should be available to the average person.

- **HSA**: Lastly, there's an additional pre-tax bucket called an HSA (Health Savings Account), which we'll discuss in depth in the next chapter. Limits on this plan are $3,450 for an individual plan or $6,900 for a family plan.

In all, you can contribute up to $24,000/year if you're under the age of 50, or $42,000 if you're one of the lucky individuals who have access to both a 457 and 403(b), to these tax-deferred buckets. Add in an HSA plan and you're looking at $27,450-$45,450 in tax-deferred dollars.

Properly used, tax-deferred vehicles can have a massive impact. Let's say Eliana and Jaden are married with one kid and each make $64,000/year. If neither contributes to any retirement vehicles, they'd be looking at gross income of $128,000/year. After the standard deduction of $24,000, their taxable income would be $104,000. This means their tax burden is $14,759. After the child tax credit, they'd be looking at a total tax bill of $12,759.

Now let's say Elaina and Jaden max out their 401k, IRAs and an HSA family plan. Through this, their $128,000 of income would drop to $73,100. After the standard deduction, they'd be looking at taxable income of $49,100. This means their tax burden is $5,511. After the child tax credit, they'd be looking at a total tax bill of $3,511. This is a **$9,248** difference!

Now, what if Elaina & Jaden maxed these plans out for ten years and had absolutely no pay raises? Each year, they took the $9,248 saved from taxes and put it into VTSAX. Assuming a 7% real return (that is, adjusted for inflation), they'd have **$133,913.57** after ten years.[97]

"Hold on," some of you might say, "these accounts are tax-deferred, meaning you'll still need to pay taxes on them when you withdraw the funds." Yes, and to boot, you can't access these funds

---

[97] "Compound Interest Calculator" *U.S. Securities and Exchange Commission*, last modified August 25, 2016, https://www.investor.gov/additional-resources/free-financial-planning-tools/compound-interest-calculator

until you're in your 60's unless you want to pay the dreaded 10% early withdrawal penalty.

This is when the *Roth conversion ladder* comes in. This method allows you to take out tax-deferred funds early and, if played correctly, with little to no tax burden. Through this method, you'll be able to contribute tax-free and withdraw tax-free without the 10% early withdrawal penalty much earlier than age 65.

When this method was discovered by The Mad Fientist,[98] it set the FIRE community, well, on fire. The impact over the long term can be hundreds of thousands of dollars, as shown above. We'll discuss how to execute this strategy in chapter 22. Just know this: pre-tax buckets can easily become *no*-tax buckets, sharply accelerating your journey to FIRE.

And on that bombshell, let's discuss the best pre-tax bucket of all: The HSA.

---

[98] "How to Access Retirement Funds Early" *The Mad Fientist,* last modified July 12, 2016, https://www.madfientist.com/how-to-access-retirement-funds-early/

Chapter 19

The HSA

The HSA account was built to work in conjunction with a HDHP (High-Deductible Health Plan), commonly referred to as catastrophic insurance. Before the Affordable Care Act was passed, the HDHP was the go-to plan for the early retiree. Through an HDHP, you end up paying a lot more out of pocket than you would with a standard plan for checkups, treatments and medical services. Doctor visits wouldn't just be a $25 copay but would often cost a lot closer to the "retail" price. The benefit of the HDHP was that although you paid out of pocket for regular checkups and treatment (preventative care, however, is typically fully covered by these plans at no cost to you), should you develop a high-cost condition that incurred "catastrophic" costs, the HDHP would foot the bill. Because these high-cost scenarios didn't happen too often, monthly premiums could be found at significantly lower costs than other more traditional health insurance plans not attached to an employer.

The government recognized the higher out-of-pocket costs for these plans, so health savings accounts, or HSAs, were created. These plans allowed individuals to contribute pre-tax dollars to a designated account to be used to offset the higher cost of standard care. Since the Affordable Care Act was passed however, HDHPs have become much less popular on the individual market because they don't meet ACA requirements for the individual mandate (meaning you would still be fined for purchasing them). With the recent repeal of the individual mandate though, we could see a comeback of these plans to the open marketplace.

While HDHPs are not as widely used on the open *individual* market, more employers have started implementing them. As you can see from the below chart, 3% of employees were covered in a HDHP in 2006.[99] Ten years later, that figure jumped to 29%.

HDHP plans have been rising in popularity, and for good reason. As mentioned above, with a HDHP, you have access to the HSA. As of 2018, you can contribute $3,450 each year towards it as an individual or $6,900 if two or more are covered under the plan. Why are HDHP plans and by extension, HSAs, becoming more popular? We see five reasons:

1) **Contributions to your HSA are made with pre-tax dollars and all withdrawals are tax-free, as long as they're withdrawn to pay for appropriate medical costs.** This means you can contribute $2,000/year into your HSA and if you happen to have $2,000 of out of pocket medical and dental costs for that year, you can withdraw that $2,000 and use it pay for your medical bills tax-free. With a traditional plan, that $2,000 (though it would likely be less) would need to be paid for with after-tax dollars.

2) **Employers often match contributions to your HSA up to a certain dollar point or may pay for your monthly premiums altogether.** This is because HSA plans cost an employer a lot less. The Kaiser Family foundation ran a 2017 survey that interviewed over 2,100 non-federal public and private firms.

They found that for traditional PPO plans, employers typically pay $5,653/year for single coverage premiums and $13,430/year for family coverage. For HDHP plans, employers

---

[99]Bruce Lee, "Mercer Survey: Health Benefit Cost Growth Slows to 2.4% in 2016 as Enrollment in High-Deductible Plan Climbs", *Mercer*, last modified October 26, 2016, https://www.mercer.com/newsroom/national-survey-of-employer-sponsored-health-plans-2016.html

typically paid $5,004/year for single coverage premiums and $12,982 for family coverage.[100] Additionally, starting in 2020, employers will be taxed for offering plans with really great benefits. This tax is found within the Affordable Care Act and is often referred to as the "Cadillac tax."[101] At the moment, it's set at 40%. We can reasonably expect that the closer we get to this tax, more employers will implement incentives to get their employees on HDHPs.

3) **If your contributions are made through your employer, those contributions are also FICA-free**. In addition to paying no federal income tax, payroll contributions will avoid the FICA tax. These two programs (Social Security and Medicare) typically eat away 7.65% of your pay.

4) **Premiums and overall costs are less in comparison with a traditional health insurance plan**. Running with the same Kaiser Family Foundation study findings,[102] the monthly premium average for a single-employee on the HDHP comes out to $85/month, compared to $109/month for a traditional plan. For families, the premium average on HDHPs comes out to be $383.25/month, compared to $504.17/month for a traditional plan. And as premiums continue to skyrocket (we've seen a 55% increase in premium costs for family coverage since 2007), the incentives for a lower premium plan grow ever more appealing. This is especially true for younger individuals or those who don't visit the doctor often.

---

[100]"2017 Employer Health Benefits Survey", *The Henry J. Kaiser Family Foundation*, last modified September 19, 2017, https://www.mercer.com/newsroom/national-survey-of-employer-sponsored-health-plans-2016.html
[101]"Affordable Care Act Tax Provisions", *IRS*, last modified August 27, 2017, https://www.irs.gov/affordable-care-act/affordable-care-act-tax-provisions
[102]"2017 Employer Health Benefits Survey", *The Henry J. Kaiser Family Foundation*, last modified September 19, 2017, https://www.mercer.com/newsroom/national-survey-of-employer-sponsored-health-plans-2016.html

On average, an HDHP plan costs less for the employee—nearly $3,000 less, according to Kaiser.[103]

5) **Overall healthcare costs are lower, even for years where a major expense like pregnancy is incurred.** In September 2016, Georgi was a couple weeks away from her due date and open enrollment was upon us. We were debating whether we should go with the HSA plan or traditional PPO plan and which would result in the lowest cost. With the baby due soon, we knew we had a high-cost year ahead. At first glance, you may assume that since we were expecting a large healthcare expense (delivery), that a traditional PPO plan is the only way to go.

That's what we thought, too, until we looked at the numbers. While we can't get into specifics to protect Cody's employer's privacy, we can say that the annual premium for the HSA family plan was thousands of dollars below the middle-line PPO option. We'd have a higher deductible and higher out of pocket costs, sure; but we projected that when taking the lower premium, HSA match, and tax savings into account, we'd be better off going with the HSA plan. Our projections showed that as long as the total cost of delivery was below $40,000, that we'd end up paying less with our HSA plan over the course of a year.

Additionally, HDHP providers will often have negotiated retail rates for various procedures and medications, which surprised us with an even lower bill. Although you may think you have to pay the retail value of $80 for that prescription out-of-pocket, your "negotiated retail price" may end up being at or below the corresponding copay of a traditional PPO plan! This is what our analysis looked like, with actual rates slightly altered (again, to protect Cody's employer's privacy), based on four different cost scenarios for the baby:

---

[103] "2017 Employer Health Benefits Survey", *The Henry J. Kaiser Family Foundation*, last modified September 19, 2017, https://www.mercer.com/newsroom/national-survey-of-employer-sponsored-health-plans-2016.html

Health Insurance Cost Projections 2016
(Employer match for HSA contribution removed from HSA premium.)

Scenario #1 ($10,000 cost)	Premium Plan	Balanced Plan	HSA
Annual Premiums	$7,200.00	$4,800.00	$2,400.00
Deductible	$750.00	$3,000.00	$3,000.00
Remaining Retail Costs After Deductible	$9,250.00	$7,000.00	$7,000.00
Coinsurance	$925.00	$1,400.00	$1,400.00
Increased FICA Costs	$550.80	$367.20	$0.00
Total Costs	**$9,425.80**	**$9,567.20**	**$6,800.00**

Scenario #2 ($20,000 cost)	Premium Plan	Balanced Plan	HSA
Annual Premiums	$7,200.00	$4,800.00	$2,400.00
Deductible	$750.00	$3,000.00	$3,000.00
Remaining Retail Costs After Deductible	$19,250.00	$17,000.00	$17,000.00
Coinsurance	$1,925.00	$3,400.00	$3,400.00
Increased FICA Costs	$550.80	$367.20	$0.00
Total Costs	**$10,425.80**	**$11,567.20**	**$8,800.00**

Scenario #3 ($30,000 cost)	Premium Plan	Balanced Plan	HSA
Annual Premiums	$7,200.00	$4,800.00	$2,400.00
Deductible	$750.00	$3,000.00	$3,000.00

Remaining Retail Costs After Deductible	$29,250.00	$27,000.00	$27,000.00
Coinsurance	$2,925.00	$5,400.00	$5,400.00
Increased FICA Costs	$550.80	$367.20	$0.00
Total Costs	**$11,425.80**	**$13,567.20**	**$10,800.00**

Scenario #4 ($40,000 cost)	Premium Plan	Balanced Plan	HSA
Annual Premiums	$7,200.00	$4,800.00	$2,400.00
Deductible	$750.00	$3,000.00	$3,000.00
Remaining Retail Costs After Deductible	$39,250.00	$37,000.00	$37,000.00
Coinsurance	$3,925.00	$7,400.00	$7,400.00
Increased FICA Costs	$550.80	$367.20	$0.00
Total Costs	**$12,425.80**	**$15,567.20**	**$12,800.00**

As you can see, even up to a cost of $40,000, the HSA plan would be the most cost-effective option.

HDHP plans that come with an HSA not only offer strong tax incentives but can also end up costing you less, even with a major expense like birth. If this is where the chapter ended, we'd hope we convinced you that HDHP is the way to go. The HSA has even more to offer, though.

Contributions made to an HSA account don't just have to sit there, being eaten away by inflation. If you login to your HSA portal, you'll find you actually have the option of investing your contribution balance, often in low-cost index funds. Your HSA account acts as its own mini-retirement account!

Ah, but you might think that you can only use those funds for medical expenses, or else you'll get hit with taxes. And you'd be right. In fact, not only will you get hit with taxes, you'll also pay a **20%** early withdrawal fee. *However*, once you turn 65, you can use those funds for whatever you want without paying that early withdrawal fee. And since early retirement includes standard retirement (e.g. after age 65), you can count your HSA balance towards your Number and can focus on maxing out your contributions! Odds are you will have somewhat regular medical expenses for which this can be used before 65, and those expenses will likely increase with age. Then when AARP starts sending you love letters, you can withdraw as much as you need for any expense.

Since your HSA account isn't tied to your employer, you can also use contributions towards medical expenses incurred even after you leave your job. To reiterate, *if you have a balance of $50,000 in your HSA account, you can use that full balance, plus whatever it returns, on medical expenses for the rest of your life.*

We've shown that all contributions to your HSA are free from federal tax and FICA tax and that you can withdraw contributions to pay for qualifying medical costs without penalty or tax. So, say you get a bill for $200 from your doctor's office for treating a sprained ankle and need to pay it. You have two options at this point. First, you can use your HSA card to pay the bill, which is like a debit card tied to your HSA balance. Or, you can use your credit card to rack up some credit card points and reimburse yourself, as long as you keep the receipt.

The HSA Reimbursement Hack

That last option regarding reimbursements got some clever early retirees thinking.[104] Is there a time-limit in which you must reimburse yourself for a medical expense, or can you hold off on

---

[104] "HSA - The Ultimate Retirement Account", *Mad Fientist,* last modified October 17, 2012, https://www.madfientist.com/ultimate-retirement-account/

reimbursing yourself? The answer is no. *The IRS has no time limit on reimbursing yourself*, meaning if you're 30, this $200 bill can be reimbursed to you at age 70 as long as you keep the receipt.

You might think, "Why wouldn't you want to reimburse yourself right away though? If you don't, won't inflation eat away at that $200 and by age 70, wouldn't that be worth a box of cereal?" Well, if your balance just sat in your account without earning anything, yes. But by not reimbursing yourself, that $200 can stay in your account and stay invested in index funds. Since we know average returns are 7% after inflation, your tax-free contribution will most likely grow and grow and once you turn 65, you can pull your $200 plus all the interest it generated over the years. Or if you find yourself in a situation where you need some capital prior to age 65, you can start reimbursing yourself for all the medical expenses accrued since you've had your HSA account. You do, unfortunately, need to keep your receipts. But if you're a somewhat organized person, the reward is worth the trouble.

To recap, an HSA account acts as a stellar tax-deferred retirement account, as it eliminates FICA tax on your contributions, will often come with a generous employer matching program, and will likely reduce your overall health insurance costs.

Chapter 20

Investment Prioritizing and Tax Harvesting

The last few chapters have covered which investment to go with (VTSAX) and which vehicles to hold those investments (401k, HSA, IRA, taxable brokerage account). You're funding these vehicles with the surplus you created after cutting your expenses and paying off your debt. If you're really motivated, you should be putting as much as you can toward these vehicles, hopefully maxing them out - meaning, contributing up to the pre-tax limit.

The first question we'll address in this chapter is this: what if you don't have enough of a surplus to max out your 401k at $18,500, your IRA at $5,500, your HSA at $3,450 and fund your taxable brokerage account? Which should you prioritize?

We've already established that the priority should be on pretax vehicles, which means if you're single and you can only invest $25,000/year, you shouldn't be funding your after-tax brokerage account at all. These are the order of operations in which you should invest:

Match 401K	Max HSA	Max IRA	Max 401K	Taxable

1) **Get the full 401K match.** Invest in your 401k, just enough to get the company match. This is *free money*. Don't pass up free money! If you make $60,000 and your employer matches up to 5% of your salary, you need to contribute $3,000 to get the maximum match.

2) **Max out your HSA.** Next, max out your HSA. Not only is this tax-deferred, but you don't pay FICA tax, making it more valuable than a 401k and IRA. Plus, you can pull the funds tax-free anytime for qualifying medical expenses. So, after the 401K match, your next $3,450 will go towards this.

3) **Max out your IRA.** While the tax benefits between your IRA and 401k are the same, you have complete control over your IRA and can set it up through Vanguard and its VTSAX fund with its annual 0.04% ER. Your 401k, on the other hand, is at the mercy of your HR team and may not have Vanguard offerings. The cheapest index fund might come with an annual ER of 0.25%, if there are any index funds at all. Because of this, your next $5,500 available dollars should go towards your IRA. If your 401k has Vanguard funds with similar expense ratios to admiral shares, though, feel free to max it out before maxing out your IRA.

4) **Max out your 401K.** Once you've contributed enough to get the match from your employer in your 401k, then promptly maxed out your HSA and IRA, return to investing in the 401k and max it out. Remember, you can contribute up to $18,500/year to this account. If you're a public/federal employee, you'll also have a 457 in addition to your 403(b), allowing you to contribute $37,000/year between the two. If you have these offerings, max them out next.

5) **Contribute to your after-tax accounts**: Lastly, after maxing out your HSA, IRA and 401k, put whatever remaining money you have into your taxable brokerage account with Vanguard (we'd recommend the VTSAX fund).

There you have it. That's the order in which you should invest. Of course, you need to pay off your debt before you start to invest, but even if you're in the middle of debt payoff you should at least contribute enough to your 401k to get the match. Even if you have an interest rate of 30% on one of your loans, contributing to get the match doubles your investment immediately, so it's always going to be worth it.

Tax-loss harvesting

These pre-tax vehicles are the best way to reduce and potentially eliminate your tax burden, but we haven't yet discussed any tax strategies you can implement on your taxable brokerage account. That brings us to the next two questions: how do you mitigate losses in the market and how do you optimize gains?

We'll address the former question with tax-loss harvesting. *Tax-loss harvesting is the process of selling an investment at a lower basis than what you bought it for, then deducting the loss off your tax liability.*

Let's say VTSAX costs $65/share when you purchase 1,000 shares of it. A few months later, it drops to $60/share. This means your cost basis has been lowered by $5/share, meaning you've had a capital loss. If you sell those 1,000 shares, you'd log a capital loss of $5,000. Come tax time, you can deduct up to $3,000 in capital losses off your income. In this example, though, you still have $2,000 of losses you couldn't deduct. Fear not, as *you can carry over those losses to the next tax year.* Although it's capped at $3,000 per year, if you logged $15,000 of capital losses, you can take that $3,000 deduction for the next five years. *

The Wash Rule

You'd probably expect us to say you should sell your shares to lock in your tax deduction and then immediately buy back in, so you don't lose any time in the market. However, the IRS has a "wash rule" that states that if you sell a stock at a loss and within 30 days of the sale, purchase a "substantially identical stock," that this loss doesn't count for the deduction.[105]

---

*Remember that credits and deductions aren't the same thing. Credits are dollar for dollar reimbursement off your tax burden, but deductions

So, what you need to do is buy a stock that doesn't trigger this wash rule. As of the time of this writing, the VTSAX (Vanguard Total Stock Market Index Fund) and the VFIAX (Vanguard 500 Index Fund) are considered different enough to not be considered a wash. Procedurally, you'd sell VTSAX for a loss and immediately buy back VFIAX shares. After 30 days, you'd then trade back to VTSAX. Through this, you don't lose any time in the market and you can lock in those capital losses to reduce your taxable income. This strategy works whether you're in the wealth-building stage or wealth-sustaining stage. If you have funds in a taxable brokerage account that experienced a loss, you can lock in this tax reduction.

Tax-gain harvesting

Tax-gain harvesting is when things get a little more complicated. If you hold a share for over a year and sell it, it qualifies for long-term capital gains tax. This tax is 0% for gains up to $38,600 if you're single or $77,200 if you're married, but these amounts are reduced by your Adjusted Gross Income and Qualified Dividends.[106] This means you can sell capital gains up to these limits to lock in your increased basis and pay no additional tax.

Let's go back to the above example of purchasing 1,000 shares of VTSAX at $65/share. Only this time, a year later, the shares are worth $75 each. Since your share price jumped $10, you have a capital gain of $10,000.

---

reduce the amount of income you have to pay taxes on. So, for example, a $3,000 deduction in the 25% tax bracket means you save $750.

[105] "Fast Answers - Wash Sales", *U.S. Securities and Exchange Commission*, last modified November 17, 2016, https://www.sec.gov/answers/wash.htm

[106] Matthew Frankel, "Your Guide to Capital Gains Taxes in 2018", *The Motley Fool,* last modified December 22, 2017, https://www.fool.com/taxes/2017/12/22/your-guide-to-capital-gains-taxes-in-2018.aspx

Next, you'd sell those shares to lock in your gain and log it as $10,000 of long-term capital gains. Come tax time, you pay $0 on this gain, as long as you're under the $38,600/$77,200 cap. This means that if shares drop to $70 a few months later, you can proceed with tax-loss harvesting, but had you not done this initial tax-gain harvesting, the $70 would be considered a gain over your initial cost basis of $65/share.

This allows you to raise your cost basis every year the market goes up without paying any additional tax (up to the amounts discussed above), so that when the market inevitably goes down, you have a tax break waiting for you after harvesting your "losses." It's a bit like climbing a ladder with the floor below you rising with each step so you can only fall so far.

It's critical to remember that you **must hold the shares you intend to sell for at least a year** to qualify for long-term capital gains tax. If the shares have been held for less than a year and you sell them, then this gain falls under ordinary income.

As you can see, these two harvesting methods can dramatically reduce your tax burden both during the buildup phase and during the maintenance stage, shortening your journey to FIRE and smoothing out your post-FIRE experience.

Chapter 21

How Long will it Take to Hit my Number?

Ah, the all-important question. Mr. Money Mustache (MMM) wrote a popular article in early 2012 called "The Shockingly Simple Math Behind Early Retirement."[107] He posited that the length of your working career can be decided with one factor: your savings rate, as a percentage of your take-home pay, using a chart on networthify.[108]

While we agree with his basic claim, using the formulas as laid out by MMM might make your working career look longer than it probably will be. MMM doesn't consider two very important features that will help you get a more accurate estimate of how long it will take you to reach your Number:

1) The Adjusted Safe Withdrawal Rate
2) Post Retirement Expense Adjustments

Assuming a steady 4% SWR and that your retirement expenses will remain the same as your current expenses, you might project a journey that's a bit longer than you'd hoped. And that could really bum you out. Here we lay out a modified process; it's a little more involved, but it should give you a more accurate timeline.

---

[107] Peter Adeney, "The Shockingly Simple Math Behind Early Retirement", *Mr. Money Mustache,* last modified January 13, 2012, http://www.mrmoneymustache.com/2012/01/13/the-shockingly-simple-math-behind-early-retirement/

[108] "When can I retire?", *Networthify*, last modified May 5, 2013, networthify.com/calculator/earlyretirement

First, you need to find what your **gross savings** are. This includes the following:

- Employee & Employer 401k Contributions
- Employee & Employer HSA Contributions
- IRA Contributions
- Taxable Contributions
- Mortgage Principal Contributions

Next, you need to find your **gross income** and remove any taxes from this figure. If you made $65,000, but paid $5,000 in taxes, you'd want to use the adjusted $60,000 figure. You'd then divide your gross savings by this adjusted income to come out with your take-home savings rate. If your savings add up to $35,000 and your adjusted income is $60,000, your savings rate would be 58.33%. As you can see from the below example, utilizing tax-advantaged accounts has a major impact on your savings rate. The two charts below show a couple with the same income, but when utilizing tax-advantaged accounts, their savings rate can jump 3%!

Savings Rate Without Utilizing Tax-Advantaged Accounts	
Gross Income	$100,000.00
401k Contribution with 5% Match	$0.00
Traditional IRA Contribution	$0.00
HSA Contribution	$720.00
Expenses	$30,000.00
FICA Tax	$7,650.00
Federal Tax	$6,739.00
After-Tax Savings	$56,111.00
Gross Savings	$56,831.00
Adjusted Income	$85,611.00

| Gross Savings | $56,831.00 |
| Savings Rate | 66.38% |

Savings Rate Utilizing Tax-Advantaged Accounts	
Gross Income	$100,000.00
401k Contribution with 5% Match	$19,425.00
Traditional IRA Contribution	$11,000.00
HSA Contribution	$6,900.00
Expenses	$30,000.00
FICA Tax	$7,177.23
Federal Tax	$2,457.40
After-Tax Savings	$25,185.37
Gross Savings	$62,510.37
Adjusted Income	$90,365.37
Gross Savings	$62,510.37
Savings Rate	69.18%

Now that you know how to calculate out your savings rate, this is where our process will differ from the method laid out by MMM. You can actually use the same calculator on networthify to project your timeline to retirement. It can be found here: https://networthify.com/calculator/earlyretirement. However, you only need to complete three of the fields on the calculator:

Current Savings Rate: Enter your take-home savings rate, as discussed above.

Annual return on investment: Go with 7% here, which is the average historical inflation-adjusted return.

Withdrawal Rate: 4% is the benchmark, but we need to adjust this if 1) you're using an adjusted SWR because you have a mortgage or 2) if your post retirement expenses will differ from your current expenses. Let's look at both factors in more detail:

1) If you have a mortgage you plan on keeping for its whole term, use your adjusted SWR instead of the 4% value in this field. As a recap, if your principal and interest balance represent 33% of your expenses, you'd want to use an adjusted SWR of 4.66% (67% of 4%+33% of 6%).

2) If your post retirement expenses differ from your current expenses, divide your projected expenses by your current expenses to find the difference as a percentage. For example, if your current expenses are $30,000/year and your post retirement expenses are projected to be $25,000, take $25,000 divided by $30,000 to come up with this percentage: 83.33%. Once you have it, take the 4% SWR and divide it by this percentage. In this case, the SWR will increase to 4.80%. If you project your post retirement expenses to be above your current expenses, say $35,000 compared to $30,000, the withdrawal rate you'd want to use would be 3.42%.

Plug these three values in and get your results! If you already have an existing portfolio balance, you will need to complete the remaining fields on the calculator.

Let's run a few examples with the above parameters:

1) John is single and is in the tech field making $110,000/year with a $30/month HSA employer contribution and a 5% 401k match. He maxes out tax-advantaged accounts and has annual expenses of $20,000. He projects his post retirement expenses to be $35,000, as he hopes to eventually marry and start a family. His savings rate is 78.87%. It will take John 8.8 years to retire.

2) Emily and Josh each have jobs that pay $30,000, for a combined household income of $60,000. Emily gets a $60/month HSA match on a family plan but has terrible 401k options. Josh has great 401k options through Vanguard and gets a flat 5% salary contribution from his employer to his 401k. They don't make enough to max everything out, but they put everything they can towards tax-advantaged vehicles. They don't have children and don't plan to. They live on $25,000/year and plan to sustain that number after retirement. Their savings rate is 58.43%. It will take them 12 years to retire.

3) Jacob and Ashley make a combined income of $120,000/year with a $60/month HSA employer contribution and a 5% 401k match and have one child. They max out tax-advantaged accounts and have annual expenses of $30,000, which they plan to sustain post-retirement. They also have a mortgage they plan to keep with principal+interest payments representing 33% of their annual expenses. Their savings rate is 72.71%. It will take them 6.6 years to retire.

4) Jessica and Paul make a combined income of $80,000/year with a $60/month HSA employer contribution and a 5% 401k match. They have no children and don't plan to have any in the future. They max out tax-advantaged accounts and have annual expenses of $30,000, which they plan to reduce to $25,000 post-retirement. Their savings rate is 60.78%. It will it take them 9.8 years to retire

We can't possibly run examples for every scenario out there and chances are a scenario closely resembling yours wasn't covered here. But since you now know how to calculate your savings rate and can project your post-retirement expenses, simply go to networthify and plug in your numbers to see where you fall.

If you've implemented the cost cutting techniques discussed in this book and take full advantage of tax-deferred vehicles, there's a good chance you can hit FIRE within ten years of starting the journey. This may take more or less time depending on your income, post-retirement projected expenses, savings rate and debt level, but if you focus on upping that savings rate by increasing your income and/or reducing your expenses, you'll be there before you know it. Remember, we started our journey with $83,000 of consumer debt and low paying jobs. Our household income still hasn't hit six figures, but we are still on track to retire within the next handful of years. It can be done with diligence, focus and an eye on the future.

Chapter 22

You Hit Your Number! Now what?

Let's run through what you've done or will do so far, (if you've
taken our advice, that is): You've implemented the cost-cutting
recommendations laid out in the earlier chapters of this book.
Then, you sent your surplus towards debt payoff and have no more
consumer debt. After that, you shifted your surplus from clearing
away your debt, towards low cost index funds.

Once you got your investment stream going, you calculated out
your Number by multiplying your annual expenses by 25. You then
adjusted your Number for your post-retirement projected
expenses. Once you did that, you found out approximately how
long your journey to your FIRE off-ramp will take, and then you
slammed on the gas pedal and started speeding toward your
offramp to financial independence. Just a few years in, you start to
see your money grow faster and faster and you might very well
have found that your off-ramp is coming up sooner than expected.

Almost before you realize it, you spot the exit sign just ahead.
You've hit your Number. You're officially Financially Independent
and can do *anything you want*, including quit your job. But if
you're like most retirees, you're still a little anxious about the
future and sequence-of-return risk. So, you think, "Maybe I'll work
one more year" to pad your investments and reduce some of that
risk.

"One more year" syndrome is a common affliction in the FIRE
community. We call it a syndrome because that initial thought, "I'll

just work one more year," sticks around and keeps you working one more year after that, and another year after that. The security a paycheck provides is strong; we've been conditioned since childhood to expect to work full time for around 40 years (or at least, having a spouse that does so). Plus, it might feel a little awkward when all your friends, and maybe your parents, are still working. This all makes the decision to take the off-ramp just that much harder, even if you're financially ready.

So rather than second-guessing, "Do I really have enough to retire?" ask yourself, "What if I'm working longer than I need to, and is this really what I want to be doing right now?"

Life is short. Shifting the focus toward the limited number of days you have left to spend with your family and friends and make a difference here on Earth can smooth the mental transition from the traditional work-paycheck-work cycle to FIRE. Trust the math. History has shown that even through times like the Great Depression and Stagflation, the 4% rule keeps you afloat.

To drive this home, let's go back to the 4% rule and the Trinity Study and zero in on two interesting stats: [109]

1) Portfolio success rates for a withdrawal rate of 4%, based on a 75% stock and 25% bond allocation, were at 100%.

2) Portfolio success rates for a withdrawal rate of 4%, based on a 100% stock allocation, were at 98%.

As you can see, the portfolio with a 25% bond allocation had a higher success rate than the portfolio with 100% stocks. Although the average portfolio with 100% stocks ended up with almost double the value of the portfolio that had 75% stocks, you're not

---

[109] Philip L. Cooley and Carl M. Hubbard and Daniel T. Walz, "Portfolio Success Rates: Where to Draw the Line", *Financial Planning Association*, last modified April 3, 2011, https://www.onefpa.org/journal/Pages/Portfolio%20Success%20Rates% 20Where%20to%20Draw%20the%20Line.aspx

looking to be the one who ends up with the most money. You just want to make sure your chances of success are as high as they can be, and from the Trinity Study, we know that introducing bonds lowers your risk. Throughout this book, we've recommended you put all your excess money into stocks, specifically VTSAX. This holds true during the wealth-building stage. You want your money to grow as fast as possible while you work, and your consistent paycheck hedges the risk of a very aggressive 100% stock portfolio. But once you've hit your Number, or if you're hitting your Number within the next couple years, we recommend building bonds into your portfolio.

What are bonds?

Before defining bonds, let's recap stocks. When you buy a stock, you buy a little piece of ownership in that company, or in the case of index funds, an even smaller piece of a lot of companies (like every single publicly traded company in the U.S., in the case of VTSAX). When the market goes up, it's typically because companies become more valuable or we perceive them as more valuable. When a company becomes more valuable, so does their stock. As companies grow, stocks grow with them. And usually with growth, inflation slowly increases the price across the board for various goods, products and services as more money enters the market. So, when prices in general rise, stock prices rise, too. Stocks thus act as a hedge against inflation.

Bonds, however, can be treated like loans. We won't get into the specifics here, but they have various risk factors like default risk, interest rate risk and inflation risk. That's why we recommend choosing the Vanguard Total Bond Market Index Fund (VBTLX) for its wide exposure, as it holds several different bonds with varying maturity dates and interest rates, and only includes bonds that have a low chance of default.

Bonds act as a *deflation* hedge. If we loan the government $10 via a bond that has to be paid back in ten years, and if the market crashes ten years from now, thus driving the cost of goods down (deflation), the eggs that cost us $2/dozen today might end up costing $1.50/dozen then. This means that when we get the $10 back that we loaned the government, we can buy even more with our $10, in addition to the interest payments we received along the way. Stocks, in the meantime, went down with the market crash, meaning our 100 shares that were worth $1,000 are now only worth $750.

Stocks and bonds, then, are the yin and yang of the financial market. During bull markets when the market is soaring, you'll be happy you have a lot of money in stocks. But during bear markets when the market is dropping along with the cost of goods, you'll be happy you have some money in bonds. Although a 75% stock and 25% bond portfolio won't make you as much during the booms as a 100% stock portfolio, it will hurt less during the crashes.

This is exactly why having some bonds in your portfolio once you enter the maintenance stage of your nest egg (e.g. FIRE) will slightly increase your chances of success. We think you should shoot for 100% VTSAX during the wealth building pre-retirement phase and 75% VTSAX/25% VBTLX during the wealth-maintaining post retirement phase to smooth out market volatility.

Rebalancing

Regardless of the stock/bond ratio you go with, it's important that you rebalance your portfolio once a year. This means making trades to get back to your chosen allocation.

If you start with 75% stocks and 25% bonds and the stock market jumps 20% that year, while bonds stay flat at 0% returns, your stock balance might end up totaling 85% of your total portfolio, while bonds would only represent 15%. To rebalance, you'd sell some stocks and use that money to purchase bonds until your allocation is back to 75% stocks and 25% bonds.

Rebalancing is pretty snazzy; it's a way to "time the market" without actually timing the market. When stocks have a great year and you sell some of them to buy bonds to maintain your allocation, you're essentially locking in your gains on those shares. On the flip side, if stocks have a bad year and bonds have a great year, you'd sell bonds to buy stocks while they're "on sale." While timing the market is technically a fool's errand, rebalancing allows you to mitigate risk by having a set percentage of your portfolio in stocks and bonds with the side benefit of market timing.

There is a downside, though. As they say, two things are certain: death and taxes. Rebalancing *might* complicate the latter. When you sell a stock or a bond, you log whatever gain or loss you had, creating a taxable event. Since we're all about tax optimization here, we've included a couple tips to avoid increasing your tax bill:

1) **When you need to sell shares of a stock to rebalance, make sure you've held those shares for at least a year**. When you sell a stock that you've held for a year, it qualifies for long-term capital gains tax. As discussed in Chapter 20, this tax is 0% for your first $38,600 in gains if you're single and up to your first $77,200 in gains if you're married.

   However, these amounts include your adjusted gross income and qualified dividends. This means if your earned income (from, say, a regular job) is $50,000 and you're married, you'd only be able to harvest up to $27,200 at a 0% tax rate. So, when it comes time to rebalance and you have a plethora of shares to sell, choose the shares that you've held for at least a year to keep your tax bill unchanged. If for whatever reason you're forced to sell shares you've held for less than a year, then do so in your tax-deferred accounts.

2) **When you need to sell bonds to rebalance, do so in your tax-deferred accounts (401k, IRA, HSA)**. Unfortunately, the long-term capital gains tax doesn't apply to bonds; these gains are counted as ordinary income. To shield you from having to pay tax on bonds that have logged gains during rebalancing, make sure you sell bonds that are housed

in your tax-deferred vehicles. For this very reason, *your entire bond portfolio should be kept in tax-deferred accounts.*

As an example, say you need $1,000,000 to retire and you want a stock/bond allocation of 75/25. If your tax-deferred accounts have a balance of $600,000 and your taxable account has a balance of $400,000, you'd want your full $250,000 of bonds housed in your tax-deferred accounts.

The Roth Conversion Ladder

Speaking of tax-deferred accounts, let's flesh out the Roth conversion ladder we teased in Chapter 18. There are two primary retirement vehicle structures:

1) The Roth IRA/401k is an after-tax retirement account, meaning you're taxed when you contribute money, but when you go to withdraw money after the age of 59 ½, you don't pay any tax on your contributions *or* earnings.

2) A traditional IRA/401k, on the other hand, is a tax-deferred retirement account. Your contributions are tax-free, but you're taxed on both contributions *and* earnings when you go to withdraw from the account after the age of 59 ½.

Through the Roth Conversion Ladder though, *you can withdraw funds from your tax-deferred retirement accounts without the 10% early withdrawal penalty and likely with no tax.* Keep in mind that you will need to have all of your tax-deferred balances housed in your traditional IRA (Individual Retirement Account), with the exception of your HSA balance (you can easily convert your traditional 401k account balance to your IRA balance through Vanguard's website or with a quick call to them after leaving your job).

The Roth conversion ladder (RCL) is based on an IRS rule that states you can convert contributions from a traditional IRA to a Roth IRA* and avoid the 10% withdrawal penalty if you don't touch the converted amounts for five years.[110] Technically speaking, *you still must pay tax during the year you convert contributions from your traditional 401k/IRA to your Roth IRA*. This is critical. It's still considered a taxable event. Waiting five years only waives the 10% early withdrawal penalty. You still must pay tax on whatever amount you convert, during the year it's converted.

"So, wait, I thought you said this would be tax-free?" you might ask, "Now you're saying that whatever I convert *is* subject to tax?" The answer is technically yes, but practically, no. Two things come into play here: deductions and credits, and long-term capital gains/qualified dividend tax.

Let's start with long term capital gains and qualified dividends. We've established that if you hold an investment for over a year and sell it, you pay tax on whatever gains that investment made since you bought it. If you bought 1,000 shares of VTSAX at $60 each and sold them two years later for $80/each, you'd be taxed on the gain of $20 multiplied by the amount of shares you sold. So, in this case, you'd be taxed on $20,000.

But as previously stated, if you've held those shares for over a year, *you pay a 0% long-term capital gains tax for up to $38,600 of gains if you're single and $77,200 if you're married* (of course, as we said before, these amounts would be reduced by your Adjusted Gross Income and qualified dividends).

Now, let's look at deductions and credits. If you're single without dependents, you can gain $12,000 of income and have a net tax burden of $0. Even though that $12,000 is subject to tax, after the standard deduction is applied, your tax burden nets to $0. If you're married, this amount doubles to $24,000. If you're married with

---

*If you are eligible for a Roth IRA (you make under $199,000 for married filers or $135,000 for single filers), you can contribute up to $5,500, tax-free, to your Roth account each year if you're under age 50.

[110] "IRA FAQs - Rollovers and Roth Conversions", *IRS*, last modified August 26, 2017, https://www.irs.gov/retirement-plans/retirement-plans-faqs-regarding-iras-rollovers-and-roth-conversions

one child, you can have $43,000 of income and pay nothing in Federal income tax. How?

Well, after the standard deduction of $24,000, your taxable income becomes $19,000. Since you pay 10% on the first $19,050 of income, your tax burden would be $1,900. But after the $2,000 child tax credit, you'd be left with a $0 balance. The more kids you have, the more income you can have with a $0 tax burden.

So, we know two things at this point that will help us reduce our tax burden:

1) You can have up to $43,000/year in income and pay $0 in tax if you're married with one child.

2) You can also have up to $58,200/year in long term capital gains if you're married with one child ($77,200-(AGI=$43,000 income-$24,000 standard deduction)) and end up with a tax burden of $0.

Now that we know this, we can build our ladder. This is getting a little complicated, but stick with us. We promise it will pay off.

We've established that converting money from a tax-deferred traditional IRA to a Roth IRA counts as a taxable event and that if you let the money "ferment" for five years, you avoid the 10% early withdrawal penalty. Again, *the idea of the Roth conversion ladder is to convert money from your traditional IRA to your Roth IRA without tax and penalty.*

If you didn't make any income this year and you're married with one child, you can convert up to the $43,000 discussed above without paying tax. If you have a side business that brings in $20,000/year in profit, you'd be able to convert up to $23,000 without paying tax. Whatever money you convert to the Roth, up to $43,000 in our example, you have to let it sit for five years to avoid getting hit with the 10% penalty.

This means whatever you put in this year, you'll live on five years from now. You'll be able to withdraw it tax and penalty free via your Roth IRA. Then whatever you put in next year, you'll live on six years from now. You keep doing this until your traditional IRA balances are depleted, at which point you should only have your Roth IRA balance and standard taxable brokerage account to live on.

The obvious question is: how do you pay for your first five years of expenses while your first "batch" is fermenting?

You use your taxable account. Let's look at an example.

John and Mary are married with a toddler and have $500,000 across all their tax-deferred accounts (not counting their HSA). They also have $250,000 in their taxable account and live on $30,000/year. Their combined nest egg is $750,000, which meets the 4% rule for their $30,000/year of expenses. John and Mary retire and start their Roth conversion ladder.

We'll assume 2% inflation for this exercise. Inflation can't be neglected, unless you want to be just a tiny bit poorer year over year in retirement. If John and Mary plan to live on $30,000/year in today's dollars, they'll need to convert a little more than $30,000 during their first year of retirement to account for inflation. Five years from now, when they start to live on that amount, their $30k will only purchase $27,117.62 worth of today's products and services. So, John and Mary will always want to convert what they *expect* the purchasing power of $30k today to be equivalent in value to what they'll need five years from now.

Lastly, we'll assume 7% returns.

Roth Conversion Ladder with 7% Returns

Yr.	Converted to Roth	Traditional IRA (tax-deferred) Balance	Pulled from Taxable Acct to Sustain Expenses	Taxable Account Balance	Pulled from Roth to Sustain Expenses	Roth Balance
1	33,122.42	466,877.58	30,000.00	220,000.00	0.00	33,122.42
2	33,784.87	465,774.14	30,600.00	204,800.00	0.00	69,225.86
3	34,460.57	463,917.77	31,212.00	187,924.00	0.00	108,532.23
4	35,149.78	461,242.23	31,836.24	169,242.44	0.00	151,279.27
5	35,852.77	457,676.42	32,472.96	148,616.45	0.00	197,721.59
6	36,569.83	453,143.94	ZERO	159,019.60	33,122.42	215,009.51
7	37,301.22	447,562.79	Zilch	170,150.97	33,784.87	233,576.53
8	38,047.25	440,844.93	Nada	182,061.54	34,460.57	253,513.57
9	38,808.19	432,895.89	nothing	194,805.84	35,149.78	274,917.94
10	39,584.36	423,614.24	still nothing	208,442.25	35,852.77	297,893.78
11	40,376.05	412,891.19	goose egg	223,033.21	36,569.83	322,552.56
12	41,183.57	400,610.01	nothing	238,645.54	37,301.22	349,013.58
13	42,007.24	386,645.47	None	255,350.72	38,047.25	377,404.52
14	42,847.38	370,863.27	0.00	273,225.27	38,808.19	407,862.02
15	43,704.33	353,119.37	0.00	292,351.04	39,584.36	440,532.34
16	44,578.42	333,259.31	0.00	312,815.62	40,376.05	475,571.97
17	45,469.98	311,117.48	0.00	334,712.71	41,183.57	513,148.43
18	46,379.38	286,516.32	0.00	358,142.60	42,007.24	553,440.96
19	47,306.97	259,265.49	Nope	383,212.58	42,847.38	596,641.42
20	48,253.11	229,160.96	0.00	410,037.46	43,704.33	642,955.10
21	49,218.17	195,984.06	0.00	438,740.08	44,578.42	692,601.72

22	50,202.54	159,500.40	0.00	469,451.89	45,469.98	745,816.39
23	51,206.59	119,458.84	0.00	502,313.52	46,379.38	802,850.74
24	52,230.72	75,590.24	0.00	537,475.47	47,306.97	863,974.04
25	53,275.33	27,606.22	0.00	575,098.75	48,253.11	929,474.45
26	27,606.22	0.00	still nothing	615,355.66	49,218.17	972,925.70
27	0.00	0.00	0.00	658,430.56	50,202.54	990,827.97
28	0.00	0.00	0.00	704,520.70	51,206.59	1,008,979.34
29	0.00	0.00	0.00	753,837.15	52,230.72	1,027,377.17
30	0.00	0.00	0.00	806,605.75	53,275.33	1,046,018.24
31	0.00	0.00	26,734.62	836,333.53	27,606.22	1,091,633.29
32	0.00	0.00	55,427.66	839,449.22	0.00	1,168,047.62
33	0.00	0.00	56,536.21	841,674.45	0.00	1,249,810.96
34	0.00	0.00	57,666.94	842,924.73	0.00	1,337,297.73
35	0.00	0.00	58,820.28	843,109.18	0.00	1,430,908.57
36	0.00	0.00	59,996.68	842,130.14	0.00	1,531,072.17
37	0.00	0.00	61,196.62	839,882.64	0.00	1,638,247.22
38	0.00	0.00	62,420.55	836,253.87	0.00	1,752,924.52
39	0.00	0.00	63,668.96	831,122.69	0.00	1,875,629.24
40	0.00	0.00	64,942.34	824,358.94	0.00	2,006,923.29
41	0.00	0.00	66,241.18	815,822.88	0.00	2,147,407.92
42	0.00	0.00	67,566.01	805,364.47	0.00	2,297,726.47
43	0.00	0.00	68,917.33	792,822.65	0.00	2,458,567.32
44	0.00	0.00	70,295.67	778,024.56	0.00	**2,630,667.04**

As you can see, John and Mary live off their taxable brokerage account during the first five years of retirement, while their first conversion batch is fermenting. Once it's ready to go, they'll stop pulling from their taxable account and will start living off their conversion from five years prior. This allows their taxable brokerage account balance to grow through average returns, and their Roth balance continues to grow beyond the money they're pulling from it to live on. By the time their Roth conversion ladder is complete (when their tax-deferred IRA balance runs out - see year 27 in the chart), they have nearly $1.6 million in their Roth and Taxable accounts. How much Federal income tax did they pay during these 30 years? $0.

As we noted above, we're getting into some advanced concepts here that will require a little planning ahead. While we typically advocate for simplicity, there are some benefits that are worth the extra work to realize. This is one of them, and it could save you thousands of dollars over your retirement.

Here are the most important things to remember when building your ladder:

1) Convert what you'll need to cover your living expenses five years from now, adjusted for inflation. You can find a dozen inflation calculators online to tell you how much your current expenses will be in five years, based off an inputted inflation rate.

2) Don't convert more than your credits and deductions will cover, else you'll be hit with a tax bill. For a married couple with a child, this is $43,000, less whatever earned income you bring in post-retirement and any tax-gain harvesting you utilize. You'll notice that as time goes on, the conversion grows beyond $43,000, but keep in mind that credits and deductions tend to increase periodically with inflation. So, by year 15 when the conversion crosses $43,000, chances are that John and Mary's credits and deductions will cover up to $50,000 of income.

3) Live off your taxable account during your first five years of retirement, while your conversions are fermenting, making sure to keep your expenses in line with the 0% long term capital gains tax rate (a max of $38,600/single, $77,200 married, less AGI and qualified dividends).

4) Never, ever, touch your conversions during their five-year fermentation period or else you'll get slapped with the 10% penalty.

A note on 72t Distributions

72(t) distributions or Substantially Equal Periodic Payments (SEPP) are another way to access tax-deferred accounts without penalty. The way this works is you use one of three predetermined methods set out via IRS guidelines to calculate an annual payout to yourself (based on factors like life-expectancy and your account balance).[111] You then get that amount every year up until you turn 59.5 or for at least five years, whichever is later.

Well, sounds like a sweet deal, right? So why aren't we advocating this?

The problem with this method is it takes away a lot of your flexibility. You have a somewhat-set figure you withdraw each year. So, in down years, you can't withdraw less and in up years, you can't withdraw more. You can change the way you calculate out your annual payout, but you can only do it once. So, this method limits a lot of the flexibility that is so beneficial to the early retiree, and that's why we recommend the Roth Conversion Ladder method instead.

---

[111] "Retirement Plans FAQs regarding Substantially Equal Periodic Payments", *IRS,* last Modified December 29, "IRA FAQs - Rollovers and Roth Conversions", *IRS,* last modified August "IRA FAQs - Rollovers and Roth Conversions", *IRS,* last modified August 26,2017, https://www.irs.gov/retirement-plans/retirement-plans-faqs-regarding-substantially-equal-periodic-payments#7

Tax-gain harvesting 2.0

We discussed tax-gain harvesting in Chapter 20 and how it can be used to reduce your tax burden during the wealth-building phase. But it can also be utilized during the wealth-sustaining stage. As established above, a married FIRE couple with one child can bring in $43,000 of income and pay nothing in federal income tax due to the standard deduction and child tax credit. Your Roth conversions and earned income would count against this number. But what if your Roth conversion and earned income for a given year in retirement only totals $33,000? That means you could've still earned an additional $10,000 of tax free dollars. Obviously, you can't just snap your fingers and increase your income by $10,000 to lock in that 0% tax rate, right? Well, tax-gain harvesting can have a similar effect.

Say you purchased 1,000 shares of VTSAX for $65/share. Only let's say a few months later, the price is now at $75/share. Since your share price jumped $10, you have a capital gain of $10,000.

You can sell those shares to lock in your gain and log an extra $10,000 of income. And since you had $10,000 of tax free room to work with, you pay nothing on this gain. Through this, you have effectively raised your cost basis from $65/share to $75/share without paying tax. This means that if shares drop to $70 a few months later, you can proceed with tax-loss harvesting, but had you not done this initial tax-gain harvesting, the $70 would be considered a gain over your initial cost basis of $65/share. You could also just increase your Roth conversion by whatever amount of tax-free dollars you have left to work with, but that could complicate your planning.

Other Considerations

The early retiree has a lot more going for him or her than a mere nest egg worth roughly 25x their expenses. Below are some other considerations that should help you breathe easier:

1) If you make it to FIRE, chances are you're a resourceful person. You've learned how to reduce your costs down to bare bones during the debt payoff phase. During down years (and recessions usually bottom out after a year or so, so this shouldn't be long-term), you can find ways to reduce your expenses to help ease the pains of a bear market. If it looks like the economy will take more than a couple years to recover, moving to an area with a lower cost of living during these down years could also reduce the risk of portfolio failure.

The chances of you never earning another penny again for the rest of your life is probably low, too. Maybe you'll start a side gig like writing a blog, doing tax prep, or building up a skill you've always wanted to learn. In any case, now that you're retired, you can do what you want, and that might include earning additional income. That income will make the ride even smoother.

2) Something we haven't brought up in this book yet is Social Security. We all contribute 6.2% (dependent on income) of our pay towards Social Security. Additionally, our employers contribute a matching 6.2%, meaning 12.4% of our collective earned income is going towards this government-run "retirement plan." According to the US Bureau of Labor Statistics, the average salary for a worker in 2017 was $44,564.[112] This means $5,525.94 went towards Social Security between the employer and employee each year, on average. Take that by the average working career of, say, 40 years, and the average person would've contributed $221,037.44.

Many young people are anxious about Social Security not being available to them when they're ready to retire, and that's a valid concern. While we do think SS payments could be

---

[112] "Table 3. Median usual weekly earnings of full-time wage and salary workers by age, race, Hispanic or Latino ethnicity, and sex, fourth quarter 2017 averages, not seasonally adjusted", *Bureau of Labor Statistics,* last modified January 17 2018, https://www.bls.gov/news.release/wkyeng.to3.htm

reduced or the age of collection might be pushed back, the odds are slim that it will be eliminated, for the simple reason that telling an average worker who contributed over $220,000 (including the employer contribution) to Social Security that they wouldn't get anything back would be political suicide. Although SS may be reduced or altered, in all likelihood you will have something waiting for you in your 60s to further smooth your journey.

3) You'll be eligible for Medicare after age 65, which will further reduce your annual expenses.

To beat a dead horse, the 4% rule itself has a very high rate of success. The rule was based off a 30-year window and counted success as any positive balance at the end of the term, regardless of how low that balance was. But on average, you should end up with multiple factors of your starting balance. And if you reduce your 4% withdrawal rate to 3.00-3.50%, your success rate goes through the roof. After adding in some of the things mentioned above, you can be about as certain of success with 4% as you can be of death (but not taxes!).

BUT WHAT *IF?!*

But what if the tax laws change? What if legislators knock the Roth conversion ladder out from under you and suddenly you're stuck paying a 10% penalty on the vast majority of your withdrawals? Or what if they *do* eliminate Social Security or Medicaid? What if the stock market *does* crash and burn and never recover?

These are all major changes we couldn't possibly cover in-depth here. Nevertheless, we will address these fears in summary:

What if the Roth Conversion Ladder is taken out of play?

Say you built up your nest egg and suddenly, they remove the tool you had been planning your entire retirement around. You have $600,000 in tax-deferred accounts and only $400,000 in taxable accounts and now feel you may not be able to touch the $600k until you're 65. Now you're kicking yourself for not going with a Roth from the get-go.

Well, let's take a closer look. We've stressed that the married early retiree should push for $30,000 in annual expenses. But let's say you settle at $40,000 in annual expenses and are married with one child. Let's also say you had a combined household income during your buildup phase of $70,000, meaning your top dollar was taxed at 12%. Had you gone with a Roth, your contributions would've been taxed at 12%. But now you're looking at needing to withdraw from your tax-deferred accounts and pay a penalty. So, you pull $45,000 and are immediately hit with a 10% penalty of $4,500. We'll call this a 10% tax.

This would leave you with $40,500, enough to cover your expenses. Come tax time, your $40,500 would be reduced by the standard deduction of $24,000, resulting in taxable income of $16,500. This falls into the 10% tax bracket, meaning you owe $1,650. But your child tax credit of $2,000 covers this completely!

So, when everything is said and done, even if they take away the Roth conversion ladder, your effective tax rate is 10% (the penalty), as opposed to 12% for what you would've been hit with on a Roth contribution. Granted, your Roth does grow tax-free, but if you access that growth before 59 1/2, you pay that same 10% penalty. So overall, you're still better off going the traditional route, even if the Roth conversion ladder is eliminated.

What if they eliminate Social Security or Medicare?

Well, thankfully, our guide doesn't count either of these when it comes to projecting your expenses for retirement and building your nest egg. So, the plan proposed and the 4% rule that backs it up already "assumes" you won't be relying on these programs. Once they get added in, it's just icing on the cake.

What if the stock market crashes and never recovers?

This is a pretty small "if." If the market never recovers, that means the entire US economy collapses. At that point, it really doesn't matter where you have your money invested. And in this situation, you'd likely have to go back to the workforce (which becomes more difficult the longer you're out of it). Ultimately, we believe this is about as likely as the sun exploding tomorrow. Things may crash and burn, but they will recover. The Great Depression is about as bad as it can possibly get here, and even if we end up going through one of these rare events again, the tactics and techniques presented in this book should get you through it.

Required Minimum Distributions

We hope this chapter helped to alleviate some of the concerns you may have when it comes time to take the off-ramp.

But we must cover one IRS rule that may hurt the early retiree once he/she turns 70 ½. This book has been all about deferring and eliminating taxes. We just went over the RCL and assumed a return of 7% before inflation while building our example ladder. But how do things change if we use the 11% the index has actually returned, before inflation? It looks like this:

Roth Conversion Ladder with 11% Returns

Yr.	Converted to Roth	Traditional Account Balance	Pulled from Taxable Account to Sustain Expenses	Taxable Account Balance	Pulled from Roth to Sustain Expenses	Roth Balance
1	33,122.42	466,877.58	30,000.00	220,000.00	0.00	33,122.42
2	33,784.87	484,449.25	30,600.00	213,600.00	0.00	70,550.75
3	34,460.57	503,278.10	31,212.00	205,884.00	0.00	112,771.90
4	35,149.78	523,488.91	31,836.24	196,695.00	0.00	160,326.59
5	35,852.77	545,219.92	32,472.96	185,858.49	0.00	213,815.29

6	36,569.83	568,624.28	0.00	206,302.92	33,122.42	240,782.38
7	37,301.22	593,871.73	0.00	228,996.24	33,784.87	270,784.79
8	38,047.25	621,150.37	0.00	254,185.83	34,460.57	304,157.81
9	38,808.19	650,668.71	0.00	282,146.27	35,149.78	341,273.58
10	39,584.36	682,657.91	0.00	313,182.36	35,852.77	382,545.26
11	40,376.05	717,374.24	0.00	347,632.42	36,569.83	428,431.46
12	41,183.57	755,101.84	0.00	385,871.98	37,301.22	479,441.26
13	42,007.24	796,155.81	0.00	428,317.90	38,047.25	536,139.78
14	42,847.38	840,885.56	0.00	475,432.87	38,808.19	599,154.35
15	43,704.33	889,678.64	0.00	527,730.48	39,584.36	669,181.30
16	44,578.42	942,964.88	0.00	585,780.84	40,376.05	746,993.61
17	45,469.98	1,001,221.03	0.00	650,216.73	41,183.57	833,449.33
18	46,379.38	1,064,975.96	0.00	721,740.57	42,007.24	929,500.90
19	47,306.97	1,134,816.34	0.00	801,132.03	42,847.38	1,036,205.59
20	48,253.11	1,211,393.03	0.00	889,256.55	43,704.33	1,154,736.99
21	49,218.17	1,295,428.09	0.00	987,074.78	44,578.42	1,286,397.81
22	50,202.54	1,387,722.64	0.00	1,095,653.00	45,469.98	1,432,634.13
23	51,206.59	1,489,165.54	0.00	1,216,174.83	46,379.38	1,595,051.08
24	52,230.72	1,600,743.03	0.00	1,349,954.06	47,306.97	1,775,430.45
25	53,275.33	1,723,549.43	0.00	1,498,449.01	48,253.11	1,975,750.02
26	54,340.84	1,858,799.03	0.00	1,663,278.40	49,218.17	2,198,205.19
27	55,427.66	2,007,839.26	0.00	1,846,239.02	50,202.54	2,445,232.88
28	56,536.21	2,172,165.37	0.00	2,049,325.32	51,206.59	2,719,538.12
29	57,666.93	2,353,436.63	0.00	2,274,751.10	52,230.72	3,024,123.53
30	58,820.27	2,553,494.38	0.00	2,524,973.72	53,275.33	**3,362,322.06**

As you can see, because returns are at 11%, even with conversions, your tax-deferred account balance just continues to grow (since your returns are greater than your withdrawals). This is through a mere 30 years. If you're retiring at 30, the 40.5-year gap to 70.5

can result in a tax-deferred balance of well over $6 million dollars. At that point, required minimum distributions come into play. This is when the government grows tired of not collecting taxes on your tax deferred accounts and starts to make you withdraw those funds and pay taxes on them in ever-increasing percentages, or else face a penalty of 50%[113] of how much you fall short on.

So, how much does Uncle Sam demand that you to withdraw? It depends on your tax-deferred account balance and your life expectancy. To calculate your RMD for the year in question, you take your tax-deferred balance from the prior year, say $2,500,000 and divide it by the IRS-defined distribution period, as shown in the table below.

Age	Distribution Period	Age	Distribution Period	Age	Distribution Period	Age	Distribution Period
70	27.4	82	17.1	94	9.1	106	4.2
71	26.5	83	16.3	95	8.6	107	3.9
72	25.6	84	15.5	96	8.1	108	3.7
73	24.7	85	14.8	97	7.6	109	3.4
74	23.8	86	14.1	98	7.1	110	3.1
75	22.9	87	13.4	99	6.7	111	2.9
76	22	88	12.7	100	6.3	112	2.6
77	21.2	89	12	101	5.9	113	2.4
78	20.3	90	11.4	102	5.5	114	2.1
79	19.5	91	10.8	103	5.2	115	1.9
80	18.7	92	10.2	104	4.9		
81	17.9	93	9.6	105	4.5		

---

[113]"Retirement Topics - Required Minimum Distributions (RMDs)", *IRS*, last modified August 26, 2017, https://www.irs.gov/retirement-plans/plan-participant-employee/retirement-topics-required-minimum-distributions-rmds

As you can see if you're 70, the distribution period is 27.4. This means when you're 70, you have to withdraw $91,240.88![114] It just gets worse and worse as time goes on.

Obviously, this is likely much more than an early retiree needs to live on. So, what are your options? Well, you can increase your Roth conversion to the point where you pay a little tax now (maybe fall into the 12% tax bracket) so your traditional balance is depleted by the time those RMDs become due. After all, 12% now is better than a 32% tax rate later. Or you can just withdraw what's required and pay taxes. Even after taxes, you're left with a huge amount of money to live on.

The other thing you can do is start a charity. JL Collins wrote a valuable article called "How to Give like a Billionaire."[115] He found that you can start a charitable foundation through Vanguard by putting in as little as $25,000. So, if the government makes you take out $200,000 to collect their, say, 32% tax at that point, instead of "donating" $64,000 to the government, donate the extra money you don't need to live on to your charitable foundation so your money goes to where you want it to go instead of the government (unless you want it to go to the government—then by all means, give them whatever you want).

But regardless of how you handle RMDs, it's a good problem to have.

---

[114] "Required Minimum Distribution Worksheets", *IRS,* last modified August 26, 2017, https://www.irs.gov/retirement-plans/plan-participant-employee/required-minimum-distribution-worksheets
[115] JL Collins, "How to Give like a Billionaire", *jlcollinsnh,* last modified February 8, 2012, http://jlcollinsnh.com/2012/02/08/how-to-give-like-a-billionaire/

Conclusion

We all come from different walks in life and we're all in different situations. One reader might make six figures a year and live in the heart of a metropolitan city. Another might make minimum wage and is trying to figure out how to keep his rent check from bouncing. The beauty of FIRE is that anyone can do it if he takes home more than he spends, invests the difference, and lets time work its magic. You might not have created a surplus yet, and that's OK. Using the tools provided in this book, you can reduce your expenses to create that surplus and then invest it wisely.

Remember, this journey is like a road trip. Your destination is the Number that will sustain your lifestyle for the rest of your life. The fuel you use is low-cost index funds and as you "accelerate," your money creates money, which in turn creates more money, thus speeding up your journey to the FIRE off-ramp. You can boost your speed with nitrous oxide (maxing out tax-deferred accounts) to get you there even faster.

Though you may experience some bumps and traffic along the way, as life circumstances and market performance don't always jive well with your plans, if you continue to invest, even if it's just a little, you're making progress towards your destination. Sometimes you'll scoot along at 1 MPH while stuck in stop-and-go traffic; at other times, traffic will clear, and you'll be cruising at 75 MPH. The point is that you'll get there, as long as you generate that surplus and invest it.

Once you get there, you'll know what to do to help mitigate the sequence-of-return risks and other portfolio risks, and how to hack high cost services like college and healthcare. You know how to access tax-deferred account balances early without penalty and tax. Although your chances of success are already incredibly high when you do pull the trigger, implementing a combination of bonds, geoarbitrage, tax-loss and tax-gain harvesting, flexibility, side incomes and federal programs like Medicare and Social Security will practically guarantee not only a successful portfolio, but a portfolio that will likely be worth multiple factors of its balance a few decades into FIRE.

We hope this guide has inspired you to cut your expenses, invest your surplus and plot a course to Financial Independence. The community of early retirees is growing for a reason: FIRE offers independence and flexibility to invest in your talents and passions, explore the world, and spend more time with the people you love without the risk of burn-out or feeling tied down by the traditional paycheck.

It's never too early to start establishing your financial independence. Work hard, be frugal, invest wisely, and clock out early.

Made in the USA
Columbia, SC
13 April 2019